"A great many Americans have been searching for some new meaning in their personal lives during the past few years. You may be among them. I am.

"I am also a federal official who's concerned about the *national* consequences of our failure to provide the quality of life that would permit us to attain more of our full potential.

"No one—save fanatics and corporate profiteers— represents that he has 'the' answer. Your answer must be found for you and by you.

"At the same time, it seems to me we ought to share with each other such incomplete and imperfect insights as we've evolved. We ought to help each other. We damn sure aren't getting any help from Big Business, Big Broadcasting, or Big Government."
—NICHOLAS JOHNSON
Federal Communications Commissioner

THIS BANTAM BOOK
HAS BEEN PRINTED ON RECYCLED PAPER

To

America:
the people, the land, the dream and the
possibility it may all yet come true

I am waiting for someone
to really discover America

—Lawrence Ferlinghetti

It was the inevitability of America that stirred ... [Tom Paine] most; here was a new breed of men, not out of blood nor class nor birth, but out of a promise pure and simple; and the promise when summed up, when whittled down, when made positive and negative, shorn of all the great frame of mountains, rivers, and valleys, was freedom, and no more and no less than that.

—Howard Fast
Citizen Tom Paine

Test Pattern For Living

Nicholas Johnson

A NATIONAL GENERAL COMPANY

TEST PATTERN FOR LIVING

A Bantam Book / published September 1972

Back cover photo by Jim Palmer, Wide World Photos

iv

Library of Congress Cataloging in Publication Data

Johnson, Nicholas, 1934—
    Test pattern for living.

    Bibliography: p. 146.
    1. Mass media—Social aspects—United States.
    2. United States—Social conditions—1960-   I. Title.
HM258.J62   301.16'1'0973   72-5204

Published simultaneously in the United States and Canada

Bantam Books are published by Bantam Books, Inc., a National General company. Its trade-mark, consisting of the words "Bantam Books" and the portrayal of a bantam, is registered in the United States Patent Office and in other countries. Marca Registrada. Bantam Books, Inc., 666 Fifth Avenue, New York, N.Y. 10019.

Contents

GODSEND

Words & music (through/by) Mason Williams.

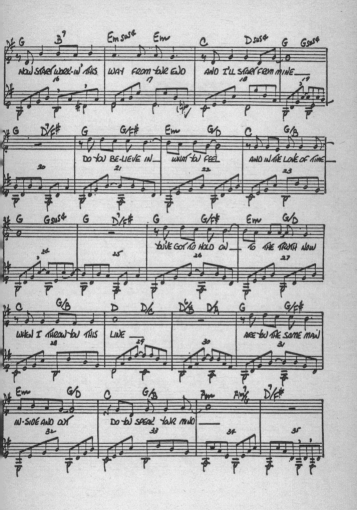

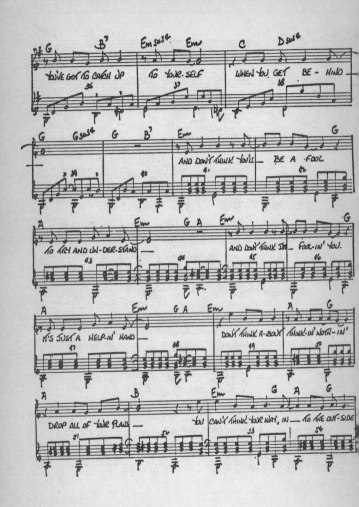

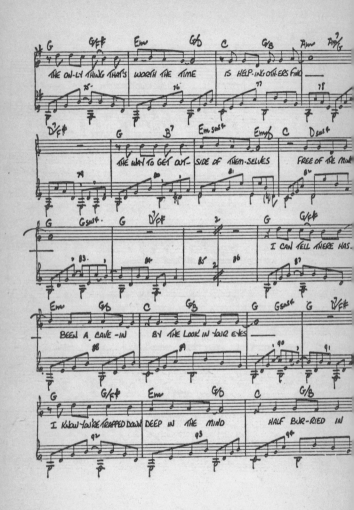

Introduction

A great many Americans have been searching for some new meaning in their personal lives during the past few years. You may be among them. I am.

I am also a federal official who's concerned about the *national* consequences of our failure to provide the quality of life that would permit us to attain more of our full potential.

No one—save fanatics and corporate profiteers—represents that he has "the" answer. The answer is that the answer changes. It is to be found, in part, in the act of searching for the answer. Your answer must be found for you and by you. You cannot buy it in a store or read it in a book.

At the same time, it seems to me we ought to share with each other such incomplete and imperfect insights as we've evolved. We ought not be shy about the personal facts of our lives just because we're unsure of ourselves. We ought to help each other. We damn sure aren't getting any help from Big Business, Big Broadcasting, or Big Government.

If I were to wait until I was qualified to write this book, I'd never be able to start it. There are lot of books I haven't read, experiences I've yet to have, and theories I haven't tested fully. Between the time this manuscript is finished and the book reaches you there will probably be a lot of things I'll want to change in it. All I can represent is that this book, when written, was intended to be honest and helpful.

Many of the ideas here are borrowed. The Greeks philosophized about—and practiced—the "balanced life." All the world's great religions have warned of materialism for centuries. Our parents and grand-parents know the value of good nutrition, walking in the woods, and so forth. It's preposterous for a person today to announce that these are truths he has personally discovered and presented to mankind.

Moreover, any honest author will admit he has drawn heavily from the writings of others. I have emphasized this fact by the use of quotations from diverse sources even though many of them came from reading I did after I wrote the text. All I can do is update these ideas a bit, give them a personal twist, and perhaps arrange them together in a way that strikes a chord in you.

Another reason I have emphasized the quotes is that my search involves the discovery of common themes in men's wisdom. When different people start saying the same thing—when a blue-collar worker expresses frustrations similar to those of college students, when the teachings of Buddha are consistent with the insights of psychiatrists, or when ecologists echo the sentiments of poets—I feel excitement. If you want, you can just read the quotes, and skip my text entirely—or read it later. (If you care about sources and citations, they're listed at the back of the book.)

My own perspective on the world comes from two directions.

My professional life has been spent as a law clerk (to Chief Judge John R. Brown, U.S. Court of Appeals, Fifth Circuit, and to the late Supreme Court Justice Hugo L. Black); as a law professor (University of California, Berkeley, and Georgetown University); as a lawyer (Covington and Burling, Washington, D.C.);

as a public official (U.S. Maritime Administrator, and Federal Communications Commissioner); and as an author (*How to Talk Back to Your Television Set*). So it is my professional responsibility to think about, and help fashion, societies that will contribute to the "life, liberty and pursuit of happiness" of their members (the *reason* "governments are instituted among men," according to our Declaration of Independence). It is not the business of government to fashion and feed the souls of its citizens, but it most certainly is the business of government to create the kind of society in which men can properly tend to the flourishing of their own souls.

The other direction to my life is personal. The usefulness to you of what I have written depends upon where you are right now—geographically, emotionally, economically, professionally, and personally. No one leads a "typical" life; each of us is different from others in a thousand ways. We've all had our own personal crises. In some ways I may have been in a better position to innovate than you; in other ways I have probably been more restricted.

During the time this book was being thought through and written, I was living alone. Because I don't have a boss, my job permits some idiosyncrasies and flexibility. Living in apartments gives me an easy choice (and change) of locations not permitted by a suburban mortgage. And my income is at least enough that my simplistic life style can be in part a matter of choice. On the other hand, I come out of a very "straight" (disciplined, achievement-oriented) background. I still have significant family ties and obligations (including that mortgage) and I have some administrative and personal responsibilities to a staff and seven-year Presidential appointment that (I felt) precluded my "dropping out." You may be less restrained.

When I write of the pressures in our society generated by Big Business, Big Broadcasting, and Big Government, it is for two reasons. I think some analysis of such pressures is necessary to an understanding of what's wrong with our lives as individuals. Otherwise it's like a fish trying to understand why he doesn't feel good in terms of physiology and philosophy, when the real problem is the polluted water in which he's swimming.

But the wisest readers will recognize that this book is as much a professional as a personal statement. As a political scientist, lawyer, and government official, I am also trying to say that these concerns—about the true quality of our lives—ought to be the business of our elected and appointed public officials. Most of the time they are not. Public officials lead bad lives just like the rest of us—maybe worse. And bad lives produce bad laws. No public official who really reads and feels what I am saying in this book could ever vote the funds to support vicious killing in Southeast Asia, or the numerous other legislative appropriations and tax schemes that rob from the poor and give to the rich. He could not fail to support increased appropriations for programs to feed the hungry, or to support the Public Broadcasting System and the arts.

John Lennon once announced he and Yoko Ono were going to send two acorns for peace to every world leader along with the suggestion that the acorns be planted. Perhaps then, he said, "They may get the idea into their heads."

I don't know if they ever did it or not. But I'm afraid all too many world leaders wouldn't get the idea into their heads—unless you "staffed it out" for them in a memo. For them this is:

"Memorandum

To: All Officials

From: FCC Commissioner Johnson

Re: Life"

For you, it's just a love poem, from Nick.

At last
New from us
This amazing dramatic proof
There.
See?
You can.
It's easy!

You mean America's favorite modern families?
Yes! . . .

Because they used that other stuff in tests
But without the special ingredient of a magic formula
Now available in two sizes
Fresh and moist
And especially made so effectively light and lovely
That the leading new word for all you ladies
Combined with their report
Is a timely message of less than a minute
And quick to fix from now on. . . .

So why not try big, tough, super
Flakes of special interest for all you guys
With twice the power and vitamins necessary
For a high rate of saturated "duh"
That is free for an unlimited time only
with every Hey!

—Mason Williams

Test Pattern for Living

Communication presupposes a community which, in turn, means a communion between the consciousness of the persons in the community.

—Rollo May

The best answer [to how to make the
citizen important again], I assume, is
to try to keep stretching people's
imaginations and concern, mainly through
the media of communication. Television . . .
has the greatest opportunity—and the
furthest to go—to widen horizons in the
arts, technology, science, societal differences, the political issues of the
nation and the world.

—Benjamin Spock

We're in science fiction now. . . . Whoever controls the language, the images, controls the race.

—Allen Ginsberg

[Broadcasting] matters more over the long run . . . than what anybody else does because [it is] more persist- ently shaping the minds of more people than all the rest of us put together.

—Archibald MacLeish

Mass Communication and Mass Disintegration

As much as the Federal Communications Commission would like to crawl back in its hole and limit its jurisdiction, the fact remains that it is knee-deep in every problem or change in our society.

Man distinguishes himself from the other animals most fundamentally by virtue of his ability to communicate—to create and manipulate symbols. However you define "communications," it ends up as part of the most fundamental and basic quality of everything that is human. Organized society at any level—whether a simple agrarian commune or a highly industrialized metropolis such as New York City—often can be most perceptively understood in terms of communications theory.

Very soon after arriving at the FCC, I came to realize that I simply could not avoid the responsibility of informing myself about the impact of radio and television programming upon virtually all of our society's problems. Ultimately these problems were going to end up at the FCC in one form or another anyhow.

- When the Kerner Commission examined race relations in the United States, it finally had to devote an entire chapter of its report to the implications of the mass media.

- After the Eisenhower Commission conducted its inquiry into violence in our country, it published two book-length staff studies on the relationships between violence in television programming and violence in our society.

- When Senator Fulbright searched for the key to the military-industrial complex, he reported his conclusions in a book entitled *The Pentagon Propaganda Machine*.

Give me the making of
the songs of a nation,
and I care not who
makes its laws.

—Andrew Fletcher, 1703

By limiting, distorting and
obscuring information, the
mass media can limit, distort
and obscure man's freedom of
action. To the extent that the
media limit his information,
they make a man less than fully
man.

—William F. Fore

It is because they [a self-governing people] are compelled to act without a reliable picture of the world, that governments, schools ... and churches make such small headway against the more obvious failings of democracy, against violent prejudice, apathy, preference for the curious trivial as against the dull important, and the hunger for sideshows and three-legged calves. This is the primary defect of popular government, a defect inherent in its traditions, and all its other defects can, I believe, be traced to this one.

—Walter Lippmann, 1922

- The most dramatic recent success in educational reform is a television program: *Sesame Street.*

- Whenever attention is focused on campaign reform, it ultimately comes back to the rising and disproportionate cost of television time and the need for free time or other solutions.

- Women's Liberation believes one of the most repressive forces in America is the portrayal of women in television programs and commercials.

An FCC commissioner in the 1970's, who is sworn to regulate broadcasting "in the public interest," cannot content himself with myopic supervision of antenna tower painting and frequency assignments. In a nation wracked by careening chaos and constructive change, he must try to evaluate whether broadcasting is part of the solution or part of the problem. And so I feel some responsibility to speculate about the root causes of the discontent in our country and to examine the possible role of mass communications in our current malaise.

What I have concluded so far has frightful implications for the responsibility of Big Business and Big Broadcasting. But it has also led me to some heartening insights about how each of us can markedly improve our own day-to-day lives in the midst of the corporate state.

Every society, in every age, has imposed some stresses and strains on the people who have lived within it. In most respects, we Americans are today an advantaged people. We complain about the burdens thrust upon us by our wealthy, industrialized society, but we are also enjoying its fruits. The medical care we receive may be inferior to that in many less affluent nations—but it is still decidedly better than that re-

Malaise and tensions are mounting throughout the world. Even affluent and strong societies show symptoms of a deep-seated uneasiness amidst uncontestable economic and technical progress. Violence has become a way of life and death when things get too complicated. Quick bloody clashes flare up almost everywhere, and nobody knows if larger confrontations are lurking just around the corner.

—Aurelio Peccei

As we talk to people across the nation, over and over again, we hear questions like these: "What does it all mean?" "Where am I going?" "Why don't things seem more worthwhile . . . when we all work so hard and have so darn many things to play with?"

The question is: Can your product fill this gap?

—a consumer products survey

Why is it that we, having everything one could wish, are unhappy, lonely, and anxious? Is there something in our way of life, in the structure or value system of our society, which is wrong? Are there other and better alternatives?

—Erich Fromm

ceived by most of the world's peoples. It's true that
our children's nutritional levels are substantially less
than our knowledge and wealth could and should make
possible. But it's equally clear that the prospect of
potential starvation is not the real specter in this country that it is for many of the nations of the world. We
may not spend our leisure time as creatively as we are
able, but we do have more time to call our own than
any preceding people in history. There is a great deal
wrong with our educational system—at every level.
Other nations have features of their educational programs that are superior to ours. But we are still, as a
nation, among the best educated people on earth.

In ironic fact, this increased wealth, education, and
leisure—the very products and prerequisites of our
twentieth-century industrialized society—now feed the
rhetoric and revolutionary life styles that challenge it.
It is important to make this point. Everything has not
gone wrong in America.

At the same time, our society—as well as that of
other highly industrialized and urbanized nations—
does take a heavy toll on the human beings who live
in it. Mostly this is something that we just feel—personally, and from our contacts and conversations with
others. But anyone studying our society today will also
uncover some very troubling statistical evidence of personal and social disintegration.

- The number of patients in mental hospitals and
  psychiatric outpatient clinics has increased 50 percent in the last ten years.

- The per capita consumption of alcohol has been
  rising since 1950; alcoholism is by all odds the
  nation's number one hard drug problem.

The fact is that they can feel better for a short time by using drugs, so it is useless to criticize them as being immoral—any more than you can criticize someone for taking aspirin for a headache. We have to help them to succeed, to get rid of the pain—or we will never reduce narcotic use.

—William Glasser

Indeed, no social emotion is more widespread today than the conviction of personal powerlessness, the sense of being beset, beleaguered and persecuted. It extends not only to Black Panthers and members of the Students for a Democratic Society but also to businessmen, publishers, generals and (as we have recently come to observe) Vice Presidents.

—Arthur M. Schlesinger, Jr.

Mr. America, walk on by
The liquor store supreme;
Mr. America, try to hide
The emptiness that's you inside.

—The Mothers of Invention

The human being cannot live in a condition of emptiness for very long: if he is not growing *toward* something, he does not merely stagnate; the pent-up potentialities turn into morbidity and despair, and eventually into destructive activities.

—Rollo May

- The number of unwanted illegitimate births per thousand nearly quadrupled between 1940 and 1970.

- Juvenile delinquency cases per thousand population have nearly tripled since 1950.

- The divorce rate has risen steadily since 1940, running as high as 70 percent in some West Coast communities.

- Suicide now ranks as the fifth leading cause of death among fifteen to twenty-four-year olds.

- A recent Harris poll indicated that 28 percent of the adult population—more than thirty-three million Americans—felt substantially alienated from the mainstream of American society.

These figures—to which more could be added—can be variously interpreted. None alone proves anything. But, taken together, they provide some evidence that a great many Americans are showing the strain, and they provide a reasonable basis for suspecting that a great many more of us are feeling pressures that show up in lesser ways. *The Wall Street Journal,* reporting primarily about and for the nation's conservative businessmen, recently revealed that many corporate executives are simply leaving their desks and going off to the woods.

But these are only the most extreme examples. Most Americans are neither statistics nor corporation presidents. They just lead dull lives which produce dull headaches. Together these people constitute the nation's most valuable, and most underutilized, national resource. For America's greatest wealth is to be found

Only within yourself exists that other reality for which you long. I can give you nothing that has not already its being within yourself. I can throw open to you no picture gallery but your own soul. All I can give you is the opportunity, the impulse, the key. I can help you to make your own world visible. That is all.

—Hermann Hesse

The gap between rhetoric and reality is so wide, the values actually operative so unrelated to biological, intellectual, and spiritual development in its fullest sense, that an authentically human existence for most Americans is an impossibility.

—Arnold S. Kaufman

The *ordinary* person is a shriveled, desiccated fragment of what a person can be.
... Our capacity even to see, hear, touch, taste and smell is so shrouded in veils of mystification that an intensive discipline of unlearning is necessary for *anyone* before one can begin to experience the world afresh, with innocence, truth and love.

—R. D. Laing

in the two hundred million man-days that are available to us every day—two hundred million days of potential productivity, potential joy, potential love, potential creativity.

The general semanticist, Alfred Korzybski, described three categories of mental health: sane, insane, and unsane. His point was that most of us, while not *in*sane, are *un*sane. We are not living up to the potential we possess as human beings. We are not fully functioning. The so-called human potential movement, including the late Abraham Maslow, argues that even the healthy human beings among us function at perhaps 5 percent of their potential.

Ask yourself how many people you know whom you think of as fully functioning personalities. How many are there in whose daily lives there is a measure of beauty, contact with nature, artistic creativity, philosophical contemplation or religion, love, self-fulfilling productivity, participation in life-support activities, physical well-being, a spirit of joy, and individual growth? That's what the world's great theologians, psychiatrists, poets, and philosophers have been telling us normal human life is supposed to be all about. But few of us have come close to realizing that potential.

There are many ways of escaping from a whole life. Suicide and the excessive use of alcohol are among the more dramatic examples. But one can also escape into work, the library, a flurry of volunteer paper work or organizational activity, sexual promiscuity, overeating, television watching, or any one of a number of hobbies.

The pressures that make us want to escape and

Society as a whole may be lacking in sanity. [Many psychiatrists] hold that the problem of mental health in a society is only ... "unadjusted" individuals. ... This book deals with ... the *pathology of normalcy*, particularly with the pathology of contemporary Western society.

—Erich Fromm

I have stayed in jail and I have stayed stupid, and I have stayed a child while I have watched your world grow up, and then I look at the things that you do and I don't understand.

I have done my best to get along in your world, and now you want to kill me. I say to myself, "Ha, I'm already dead, have been all my life."

—Charles Manson

Jesus dealt in his exorcism with the neurotic constrictions of individuals, but his whole life represented a kind of sweeping exorcism of the neurosis of a whole culture.

—Harvey Cox

I shall make little distinction
in value between talking about
middle-class youths being groomed
for ten-thousand-dollar "slots" in
business and Madison Avenue, or
under-privileged hoodlums
fatalistically hurrying to a
reformatory; or between hard-
working young fathers and idle
Beats with beards. For the
salient thing is the sameness
among them, the waste of
humanity.

—Paul Goodman

that repress our fulfillment are forces we all feel and respond to in varying ways. We are distinguished only by our capacity for adaptability, the strength of that inner force of resistance called our "individuality," and the paths we take when we are overwhelmed.

Just to say that we are living in a sick society doesn't advance the dialogue very much all by itself. It is a useful expression, however, as a prelude to—or summary of—further analysis. A great many psychiatrists and other social commentators have concluded, often reluctantly, that there simply aren't enough professional counselors available to deal with the problem one patient at a time. Besides, there's no point in curing a patient who's reacting quite understandably to intolerable pressures: he's right, it's his environment that's wrong. Is he healthier if he learns to live with such pressures? And, if not, how can a professional man in good conscience treat such a patient indefinitely? He is, almost inevitably, led to an effort to try to reform, or at least analyze, the society that is contributing so substantially to the problems of his patients.

It is revealing, I think, that the concerns expressed by thoughtful psychiatrists and social philosophers are not the exclusive preserve of a small group of liberal intellectual elitists. These concerns are also finding expression in the voices of a cross section of America: the full range of ages, educational backgrounds, social positions, races, geographical regions, wealth, job categories, and so forth. These are the people who write me thousands of letters every year. They are the people who, together, make up this country and set its course. We ought to listen to what we are telling each other and try to respond

Day after day, year after year,
climbing those same steps, punching
that time card. Standing in that
same goddamn spot grinding those
same goddamn holes.

—Ray Walczack

But there's a sixlane highway down by the creek
Where I went skinny-dippin' as a child.
And the drive-in show where the meadow used to grow
And the strawberries used to grow wild.
There's a drag-strip down by the riverside
Where my grandma's cows used to graze.
Now the grass don't grow and the river don't flow
Like it did in my childhood days.

—Joe South

with as much intelligence, imagination, and compassion as possible.

What we are telling each other has a good deal to do with television. But before we examine television, it is necessary to understand the corporate state whose cancerous growth it fertilizes.

The world is a beautiful place
                    to be born into
    if you don't mind
                    a few dead minds
    in the higher places

                            —Lawrence Ferlinghetti

We are approaching the
condition of King Oedipus of Thebes.
Thebes was a tribal society, and
when the King set about investigating
the responsibility for misery and
disorder, he found out *he* was the
criminal.

                            —Marshall McLuhan

How sharply our children will be ashamed
taking at last their vengeance for these horrors
remembering how in so strange a time
common integrity could look like courage.

                            —Y. Yevtushenko

The Corporate State

To say that the government isn't working is scarcely a partisan statement. I recall comparable sentiments being expressed during many of the past twenty years. However, the extent to which government is viewed as the problem—not just a lethargic institution incapable of effecting solutions—may be somewhat new.

There is an increasing sentiment outside of government to get on with the job. Polls seem to indicate that a great many Americans, silent or not, recognize that we have some very serious problems in our society; people are looking for leadership, and they are prepared to make some sacrifices to effect solutions. I recall a white cab driver who had been giving me some pretty reactionary complaints. On a long shot, my curiosity prompted me to ask for his solution to "the Negro problem." I braced myself for the worst, but he surprised me: "I think they have to be given better jobs and more money. A man has to have some dignity." It is my impression that, in general, we Americans are possessed of far more intelligence, generosity, good will, and common sense than our television networks and political leaders give us credit for. We need education and information—so do college professors and corporation presidents—but, once informed, our instincts are sound.

The insensitivity of our leaders has forced some Americans, however, to grow increasingly impatient and violent. This trend has been predicted by most social observers: it happens whenever a government fails to respond to the legitimate demands of its citizens. Indeed, this nation was born out of just such a violent response to intransigence in government, and the legitimation of revolution in the United States has been re-

Either out of ignorance, or out of calculated political cynicism, our citizens are being told that crime will stop if we erase the Bill of Rights—that unity will come if we suppress dissent—that racial conflict will end if we ignore racial justice—and that protest will cease if we intimidate the people who report it.

—John V. Lindsay

Mighty nations that do not respond to the needs of their own people have traditionally tried to solve problems and overcome frustrations through violence abroad and repression at home. In the process, they have hastened their own exit from center stage. The greatest security problems for a nation are the hostility and frustration of its own citizens.

—Richard J. Barnet

This country, with its institutions, belongs to the people who inhabit it. Whenever they shall grow weary of the existing Government they can exercise their *constitutional* right of amending it, or their *revolutionary* right to dismember or overthrow it.

—Abraham Lincoln

In a free-enterprise, private-property system, a corporate executive . . . has direct responsibility to his employers . . . to make as much money as possible while conforming to the basic rules of the society, both those embodied in law and those embodied in ethical custom.

—Milton Friedman

When I started teaching here [Harvard Business School] twenty years ago, everyone fully believed in the capitalist system and we started from there. Now a lot of the students not only question the system but downright distrust it.

—Thomas C. Raymond

peatedly attested to throughout our history by political leaders of virtually every political stripe.

I do not argue that the government no longer has any power. Not at all. It makes decisions that affect billions of dollars, dollars that flow from the people— as taxpayers and consumers—to the large corporations: defense contracts, agricultural and maritime subsidies, oil import quotas, natural gas rates, airline routes, and so forth.

But even though the government still has the power to act, the impetus for that action tends most often to come from the management of the largest corporations rather than from government officials. Such American corporations are larger, and more influential by almost any measure, than all but very few of the world's nations. Their management officials have a theoretical responsibility to shareholders but in practical fact are responsible virtually to no one.

There is a split in the thinking—or at least the talking—of business management today. Milton Friedman and others take the position that the only legitimate concern of corporate management is the making of money. Legitimate or not, that would appear to be the limit of the concern expressed by most corporate officials. Increasingly, however, corporate management and business-school students are expressing their uncomfortable feelings of disquiet, and they are at least talking about social responsibility.

Meanwhile, there is a growing awareness on the part of a great many people—not just young college students—that unchecked corporate greed is today more the cause of America's shame than its great pride. Large corporations tend to exert an inhibiting

I guess I just don't think it's
~~right to~~ make a profit out of killing
people.

> —Emerson Foote
> on leaving advertising agency with
> cigarette accounts

> On CBS radio the news of his
> [Edward R. Murrow's] death, reportedly
> from lung cancer, was followed
> by a cigarette commercial.
> —Alexander Kendrick

I have about reached the conclusion that, while large industry is important, fresh air and clean water are more important, and the day may well come when we have to lay that kind of a hand on the table and see who is bluffing.

> —Barry M. Goldwater

He responds, as I've explained, only to stimuli affecting his corporation. That's the thing, you see. He has totally identified with his corporation. I'm sure if you talk to him about his corporation, he'll hear and understand you and might even talk to you. Otherwise he has no sensory faculties at all.

> —Dr. Klune in Paddy Chayefsky's play,
> *The Latent Heterosexual*

When the Army killed 6,400 sheep at Skull Valley in 1968 by accidentally spraying them with VX, a deadly nerve gas, the state veterinarian, D. Avaron Osguthorpe, observed, "We've got a defense business bringing in $35 million a year into the state; sheep bring in one thirty-fifth that amount. Which is more important for Utah?"

> —Richard J. Barnet

influence on the growth and development of the human personality.

Stewardess

Business does to its women's bodies
What it does to its men's minds

It binds them tightly
Snuffing out the free
Covering with a uniform
Painting any parts that stick out
With the company colors
And a smile

Making replaceable people
With replaceable parts

Wigs and
Brains,
Inc.

These corporations also tend to be behind most of the modern-day despoiling of the air, water, and land. They tend to be, like war, "unhealthy for children and other living things." Indeed, they are more than like war, they are war. For profit can come from any enterprise. You can make more money by blowing up bodies than by treating them; the poison-gas business tends to be even more profitable than administering anesthesia. And when the only morality is measured in dollars, no appeal to human values can ever make much sense.

These corporations must manufacture and sell more and more every year. As a result, they now simultaneously create the products and the advertising campaigns to generate the market for the products: male cosmetics, electric carving knives, vaginal deodorant spray, or new brands of cigarettes. The corporations

'Cause it's one, two, three,
'What are we fightin' for?'
'Don't ask me, I don't give a damn;'
Next stop is Vietnam.
And it's five, six, seven,
Open up the pearly gates
There ain't no time to wonder why,
Whoopie, we're all gonna die.

—Country Joe McDonald

Looka here you can be like a tape deck you know
They can plug you in and you say what they want you
to say

—J. Brown, B. Byrd, R. Lenhoff

One of my very perceptive students at the University of Waterloo has said: "The adman writes the script for our lives; we read it back." He is right, but most people must know, some of the time, at some level of their consciousness, that their reading back of the script is not quite what they meant to say.

—Patrick Watson

The advertising industry will not readily give up its custodianship of our cultural life, which it has purchased with good money.

—Erik Barnouw

have tampered into destruction the genius of the free market system. The theory is that products are manufactured to satisfy preexisting needs, that the cheapest and most functional products will be selected on their merits by the consumer, and that, through his "voting" with dollars in the marketplace, the best manufacturers will prevail and profit. But once you start manufacturing needs as well as products, the whole system spins out of control—economically (inflation), socially (urban unrest), and psychologically (personality disorders).

If corporations practiced the free private enterprise they preach, there would be nothing necessarily wrong with the existence of a group of institutions and men hell-bent on profit maximizing within a society rich in diversity. There would be a sufficient number of countervailing pressures from family, church, school, the creative-artistic-intellectual community, and government to keep it all in balance.

The difficulty in America today is that we have turned it *all* over to the big corporations. Time owns Life. Our colleges, churches, foundations, and public broadcasting stations tend to be presided over by the same guys who decide what automobiles we'll buy and breakfast cereals we'll eat. They publish our children's school books; they own most of the nation's artistic talent—and they have little hesitation in censoring the copy of both.

Understanding this concept of "corporate interlock" is really essential to an understanding of this book. In general, people either understand the concept right away or not at all—in which case spelling it out is a waste of time. But I'm going to try.

Once upon a time there was a girl who dreamed of a doll that had everything. And then came Dawn, the doll that comes with these beautiful things. Like a car with Dawn actually at the wheel! Just look at Dawn go! There's a Music Box with Dawn on top, and the fabulous Dawn Fashion Show—the only one in the world with a revolving stage like this. Dawn comes with it—watch her walk and model, all by herself. And start collecting all these accessories: a handbag, elegant furniture with a phone that really works, a beauty parlor set. You can display Dawn, her friends, her fabulous clothes, right in your own home. Make your dream come true with Dawn, the doll that has so many beautiful things. Dawn's clothes are so beautiful, so stunning, so elegant, you'll want to collect more than one doll just to show them off! And it's so much fun to put two Dawns here, three Dawns there, call it "Midnight Magic." Then change their clothes, set them up, and call it "Sweet Dreams." Use your imagination! Dawn. Fun to play with, fun to collect.

—a television commercial

Free selection of a wide range of goods and services does not signify genuine freedom, particularly if the desire for these goods and services tends merely to foster more frantic work, more compulsive buying, more fear and self-doubt. In this context, free selection tends to create and sustain alienation.

—William F. Fore

One cannot successfully alter one facet of a social system if everything else is left the same, for the patterns are interdependent and reinforce one another.

—Philip Slater

Let me begin with an anecdote. One evening Mason Williams and I were debating whether to go out for dinner or cook something at his house. We finally decided we'd stay home—principally because we didn't want to bother to change clothes. This prompted Mason to start speculating—as do a great many of life's quirks.

"Nick, I've finally figured out why you have to dress up to go out to dinner."

"Why's that, Mason?" I asked.

"Because the same people who own the restaurants own the clothing stores."

His years of working for television have forced Mason to think in one-liners. (That's all you ever have time for.) And, like many of his one-liners, this one is both inaccurate in its particulars (so far as I know clothing stores are not owned by restaurateurs) and profound in its more general wisdom.

"Living" ought to be individual, spontaneous, extemporaneous; a personal quest, evolution, and growth; an experience in uniqueness. But living your life according to the corporate plan involves no more of a creative "centering," or flowering soul, than painting in numbered spaces with the indicated colors is "art." It's like putting together a jigsaw puzzle. You are living out somebody's else's plan—not yours—paying them handsomely for the privilege of doing their work for them. The psychology of acquisitiveness is to know, at every stage, what pieces you must next acquire, and in what order—house, car, sailboat. "House" takes on an externally imposed meaning: suburbs, air conditioning, grass, wall-to-wall carpeting—just as surely as "Dawn" would be incomplete without her "car," "fabulous

In America one of the basic rules many people live by is that one must keep up with the Joneses. By your own example you must turn this rule upside down. If you absolutely need a car, let it be the oldest on the block. Let your limited household appliances be virtual "antiques" and take the trouble to learn how to repair them. Claim that your wash is a bit grayer—even if it isn't—but brag that it is done without any detergent or enzymes. Save all returnable bottles, and, if you can afford it, give them to neighbors' children to redeem—it will be good training for the young and may make a few parents feel guilty.

If you are invited to parties—and you may well not be—make a point of always showing up in the same suit or dress.

At first such "odd ball" behavior will cause some embarrassment and you will hardly be popular with your neighbors. But if you manage to keep your sense of humor and patiently explain why you live the way you do, friendships and converts won't be long in coming.

Half the worry of half the people in this country is how to pay for all the brand-new and superfluous junk they have signed up for at just "pennies a day." By your example you will be offering an escape from this endless worry and if you don't lose your cool you may well move from local odd ball to local trend-setter. Keeping up with the Joneses has become such a tyranny that more than one middle-class family is ready to consider alternatives—particularly if they see a neighbor actually doing so.

—Timothy J. Cooney and James Haughton

clothes," "elegant furniture," and "beauty parlor." Sound familiar? Could it be you are now living in the doll house you used to play in? Is that an accident? It it really what *you* want?

The corporate interlock of jobs, products, and life style means that once you come into the circle at any point you find yourself surrounded by all of it. And once you're in it's very difficult to get a little bit out. The choices remaining to you are relatively meaningless—such as which color and extras you want with your Chevrolet, whether you'll drink scotch or bourbon, how "mod" your ties will be, and which toothpaste you'll use. It all fits: corporate white-collar job, suburban home, commuting by automobile, eating in restaurants, and the clothes. There is the canned entertainment of radio and television for the boredom, the bottled alcohol and aspirin for the pain, and the aerosol cans of deodorant and room freshener to maintain the antiseptic cleanliness of it all. You wear your office, your home, and your car as much as your clothes and deodorant. And from the corporate layers of externals comes your very identity—and the smothering of your soul.

Let me try another example. Once you have accepted a job in a professional or managerial capacity with one of the nation's top two hundred corporations, you will be led inevitably to the purchase of a special automatic dishwashing detergent. Here's how it happens:

You are probably working in a large, fairly new office building in a major city, and living in the suburbs. You not only feel under pressure to get a house about the same size and cost as your neighbors, but

Just as we are lowering our water table by ever-deeper artesian wells and in general digging ever deeper for other treasures of the earth, so we are sinking deeper and deeper wells into people in the hope of coming upon "motives" which can power the economy or some particular sector of it. I am suggesting that such digging, such forcing emotions to externalize themselves, cannot continue much longer without man running dry.

—David Riesman

As often as not, it seems that many of the programs and most of the commercials from Madison Avenue appeal to a set of values entirely different from, if not in clear opposition to, the set of values taught in home, in school and in the church.

—Spiro T. Agnew

A young person gets a big bang out of taking a well-paying white-collar job with a large and important company, thinks to himself "I'm making it," and sees his job as a boost to a position of importance which holds immense possibilities. He sees himself in the saddle. It's only later, much later, when the exits have all been quietly sealed off, that it becomes apparent that the saddle is really a harness, and worse, that his head is set on a completely predictable route which promises no variation from the one he has been on all along.

—Suzannah Lessard

We're like a race horse shot full of speed to make us run harder than is good for us, to win for the owners and lose for ourselves, to win the race for only the price of the chance to run.

—Mason Williams

such a house is, in fact, the only kind available. The kitchen is really quite large. It has lots of cupboard space. You may have moved a lot of kitchen stuff with you; or maybe you bought it because you and your wife never envisioned any other way to live, or because you're expected to entertain in a particular style. In any event, even though you find a camp cook set more than enough in the way of kitchenware when you're camping, you don't want all those empty kitchen cupboard shelves. Once they are filled, you feel a compulsion to use the stuff. Instead of washing a pot after it has been used, you put it aside and dirty another one. Silverware, glasses and cups, bowls and plates are likewise dirtied in great number, even during the course of a family meal, let alone when you are entertaining. Having dirtied so many pots and dishes, it really is a drag to have to wash them all by hand. So you get an automatic dishwasher. Maybe it was already in the house. Maybe you were partly influenced to buy it because the neighbors have dishwashers. But mostly you get it because you have all those dirty dishes. And once you get it, you find it's designed so that you have to use the special dishwasher detergent or the soap will suds out all over the floor. That's how, once you accept the job, you have to buy the special detergent.

Your job itself may have come about through the same kind of almost nonvolitional process. If students earn high marks in high school, they can get into "good" colleges, where they can get into "good" graduate schools if they continue in their proficiency in exam taking. If they receive scholastic honors they are offered the "good" jobs—jobs with corporations, law firms, or whatnot that are prestigious (meaning, gen-

Social custom teaches us to strive for a privately owned, single-family home in the suburbs, possessing a garage of at least two-car capacity, and filled with "conveniences" that assure us of more "leisure" time. Advertising urges us to consume and dispose. We spend much of our free time as spectators watching professional performers or in vigorous activity behind the wheel of some power-driven machine—a car, boat, or snowmobile. Life is kinetic and frantic.

Is this really what you want? The decision is yours and you are free to say no.

—Paul Swatek

The censor sits
Somewhere between
The scenes to be seen
And the television sets
With his scissor purpose poised
Watching the human stuff
That will sizzle through
The magic wires
And light up
Like welding shops
The ho-hum rooms of America
And with a kindergarten
Arts and crafts concept
Of moral responsibility
Snips out
The rough talk
The unpopular opinion
Or anything with teeth
And renders
A pattern of ideas
Full of holes
A doily
For your mind

—Mason Williams

erally, the largest). By that time you are so used to assuming that all honors are desirable and to be accepted that you accept the job with the large corporation with almost the same automatic reflex as you accept your Phi Beta Kappa key. You have internalized the standards of those about you—parents, teachers, advertisers—to the point where you may be incapable of separating your own identity from the standards of your culture.

In fact, of course, you have a little more choice than I've suggested. But an awful lot of people do end up with the automatic dishwasher detergent.

Those who are caught find that the pattern tends simultaneously to increase their anxiety, their material consumption, and their slavish dependence on the job— as well as to contribute to a waste of valuable natural resources and to environmental pollution.

The beauty is that the reverse is also true. Once you break the interlock in your own life, not only do you enjoy yourself more, it costs you less, and you're a better citizen, too.

The corporate interlock involves the unquestioned assumptions in our lives. Because they are unquestioned, and largely unperceived, it is difficult enough to describe individual examples even one at a time. But the point of the interlock is that they are not just individual examples but part of a pattern—the test pattern television is reinforcing in millions of us hour after hour.

Tell me, don't you think daytime TV is
pretty terrible?

—Richard M. Nixon

The monstrous evil of American advertising and its hold
on the mass media shames us as a nation.

—George F. Kennan

The children ranged in age from three to twelve years.
They exhibited symptoms typical of anxiety conditions:
chronic fatigue, loss of appetite, headache, and vomiting. . . .
The pediatricians discovered that the patients were spending an average of three to six hours in front of television
screens on weekdays and six to ten hours on Saturdays and
Sundays.
The parents were told to stop their children's television
viewing completely. In twelve of the thirty cases in which
the instructions were fully followed, the symptoms vanished
within two to three weeks.

—Robert L. Shayon

"Look what they've done to my brain, ma
Look what they've done to my brain
Well they picked it like a chicken bone
     and I think I'm half insane, ma
Look what they've done to my song."

—Melanie Safka

The Television Business

Of all the corporate influences in our lives, the corporate control of television is perhaps our nation's greatest tragedy. When I speak of television I am talking about the television programming that most people watch: the prime-time evening programming of the three major networks. This is not to say that the daytime programming is any better. In general it's worse. Nor is it to ignore the Public Broadcasting System, the networks' early evening news, or the occasional hours of excellence. It's just to say that television, for most Americans, means the networks' evening series programs. When 60 percent of the people say they get most of their information from television, that's the information they're getting.

It is, of course, preposterous to suggest—or even suspect—that television is responsible for everything that's wrong with America, or that it is the sole cause of any individual problem. We had social problems before we had television. We have made some progress of which we can be proud since the coming of television. But it would be equally shortsighted to ignore the findings in so many task-force reports and academic studies that link television, in greater or lesser degree, to virtually every national crisis.

Parents obviously have something to do with the capacity of their children to reach their potential as human beings—genetically and in their early environment. Television programming is not a child's only influence. But the fact remains that it is a large one. The average child will have received more hours of instruction from television by the time he enters first grade than the number of hours he will later spend in college classrooms earning a bachelor's degree. By the

Are we supposed to spend our futures grinning and watching TV all the time?

—Jerry Rubin

So they came to Jerusalem, and he went into the temple and began driving out those who bought and sold in the temple. He upset the tables of the money-changers and the seats of the dealers in pigeons; and he would not allow anyone to use the temple court as a thoroughfare for carrying goods. Then he began to teach them, and said, "Does not Scripture say, 'My house shall be called a house of prayer for all the nations'? But you have made it a robbers' cave." The chief priests and the doctors of the law heard of this and sought some means of making away with him; for they were afraid of him, because the whole crowd was spellbound by his teaching. And when evening came he went out of the city.

—Mark 11:15–19

Every time I look into the holy book I wanna
    tremble.
When I read about the part where a carpenter
    cleared the temple
For the buyers and the sellers were no diff'rent
    fellas than what I profess to be.
And it causes me pain to know I'm not the
    gal (guy) I should be.

—Gene Maclellan

Broadcasting stations should not be simply house organs grinding out the tune of big business interests which own them—and there is some evidence that this is a real danger today.

—Warren Magnuson

time he is a teen-ager, he will have spent 15–20,000 hours with the television set and have been exposed to 250–500,000 commercials. It would seem simple common sense to assume this exposure has its influence; in any event, hard-headed businessmen are willing to bet four billion dollars a year in radio and television advertising budgets on the proposition that it's having an effect, so they are effectively estopped from arguing the contrary.

We are all vaguely aware that Big Television is allied with Big Business. But you may not be aware of the full reach of that alliance. The most influential broadcasting property—talent, programs, studios, network contracts, and stations—are actually owned by Big Business, lock, stock, and barrel. Each of the three networks is a major industrial conglomerate corporation. The time on the stations is purchased by Big Business—virtually all the available programming and advertising time on seventy-five hundred radio and television stations. The entire enterprise—programs as well as commercials—revolves around the consumer merchandisers who find the medium the most effective way to sell their wares. The top talent—let alone the executives—are paid salaries that place them well up in the ranks of America's wealthiest businessmen.

There is very little that is programmed any time during the broadcast day that is in dissidence with this overall domination by Big Business. Procter and Gamble's editorial policy provides that "There will be no material that may give offense, either directly or by inference, to any . . . commercial organization of any sort. . . ." The only exceptions are tokenism: an occasional news item (carefully kept out of prime

I am of the opinion that the United States is engaged in a controversial war in Southeast Asia, and that the country has other problems, too. I think people ought at least to think about these things, but I've noticed that the radio medium is a tremendous airy goofball, which anesthetizes everyone who listens. I'm curious about the motivation of the people whose 50,000-watt pump pours such crap into the already polluted air.

—James Kunen

All of them [the television networks] have third rate news-gathering organizations. We are still basically dependent on the wire services. We have barely dipped our toe into investigative reporting.

—Walter Cronkite

In order to best serve the whole community, industry should be the voice of its intellectually and morally most advanced sector.

—Frank N. Stanton and Paul F. Lazarsfeld

When you transmit the human voice into the home, when you can make the home attuned to what is going on in the rest of the world, you have tapped a new source of influence, a new source of pleasure and entertainment and culture that the world thus far has not been able to provide with any other known means of communication.

—David Sarnoff, 1922

What I fear . . . is that by default American television is about to take . . . the road to trivialization . . . all in behalf of fifteen or twenty big sponsors.

—William Benton

time—network news is programmed as early as 5:00 P.M. in many sections of the country); or an even far rarer documentary. Even these programs are larded with commercial messages sold for as much as the networks can extract. History—the moon walk, election returns—is also "brought to you by" some commercial sponsor. Whatever the remaining benefits may be of news, documentaries, and live coverage, for those millions of American families whose television watching is limited to prime-time series shows, or soap operas during the day, Procter and Gamble's policy reigns supreme.

When radio, and then television, started, they were almost universally heralded by those in the industry as possessed of the same potential that today's "visionaries" see for them. Television was seen as an opportunity to extend the perception of the average American, to open for all the great excitement and education and self-fulfilling potential that can come from exposure to the best that man has to offer.

By now almost everyone, including those in the industry, would concede that television has failed. Not only has it failed to make of us a better race of men, it has actually made us worse than we were before. The former would be indictment enough. The latter is simply intolerable.

This national crisis has come about, in largest measure, because of our willingness to turn over our minds, and the instrument that "programs" them, to the exclusive control of commerce. What we are discovering is that the guys who are motivated to fill our sky with the smoke from their factories, and who urge us to fill our lungs with the smoke from their cigarettes,

I think television should be the visual counterpart of the literary essay, should arouse our dreams, satisfy our hunger for beauty, take us on journeys, enable us to participate in events, present great drama and music, explore the sea and the sky and the woods and the hills. It should be our Lyceum, our Chautauqua, our Minsky's, and our Camelot. It should restate and clarify the social dilemma and the political pickle. Once in a while it does, and you get a quick glimpse of its potential.

—E. B. White, 1967

[Television is] the creature, the servant and indeed the prostitute of merchandising. . . .

—Walter Lippmann

Television is a pimp for
big business.

—Mason Williams

We all understand that the public service aspects of television are somewhat exaggerated despite what they may claim because they have to be in it for the money, for the ads and so forth.

—Richard M. Nixon

When censorship is exercised at the format level no further censorship is required. It is not possible to write anything of burning importance on "Gomer Pyle" or "Green Acres."

—George Clayton Johnson

have no more concern for our minds than they have for our bodies.

If all that one could say about television is that a small group of men are getting rich beyond their wildest dreams of avarice by failing to provide the public service that the law requires from the use of public property, the matter could be dealt with on those terms. Or if it were simply a question of separating a few fools from their money in exchange for products of questionable worth, we might write this off to the hazards of any foray into the marketplace. In fact, however, it's much more serious.

There are substantial political and economic consequences that flow from the ignorance sustained and encouraged by television. When a friend of mine who is a black disc jockey was told by his first employer that he could not read the news over the station because, "You're not going to educate the nigras of this community at my expense," that was censorship with a political consequence. The same consequence flows just as surely today from the decisions of the networks' programming vice presidents—whether or not that may be their conscious motivation.

But censorship—and its effect upon a democratic republic—is just the most obvious and easily understood of television's influences on our lives. More pervasive and invidious is the anesthetizing effect and the subtle conditioning of television.

The king and the queen in their castle of billboards
Sleepwalk down the hallways dragging behind
All their possessions and transient treasures
As they go to worship the electronic shrine
On which is playing the late late commercial
In that hollowest house of the opulent blind
And I wave goodbye to Mammon
And smile hello to a stream

—T. Buckley

ANNOUNCER: Listen to Mr. and Mrs. Ken Davis tell why their 1970 Buick LeSabre is something to believe in. . . .

MRS. DAVIS: We're a young family and we're driving a Buick, and people think, well, gee, maybe, maybe you're really coming up in the world.

MR. DAVIS: This car, I think it's going to be the best I have owned.

ANNOUNCER: The 1970 Buick is something to believe in. Wouldn't you really rather have a Buick?

—a television commercial

Most advertisers were selling magic. Their commercials posed the same problems that Chayefsky drama dealt with: people who feared failure in love and in business. But in the commercials there was always a solution as clear-cut as the snap of a finger: the problem could be solved by a new pill, deodorant, toothpaste, shampoo, shaving lotion, hair tonic, car, girdle, coffee, muffin recipe, or floor wax. The solution always had finality.

Chayefsky and other anthology writers took these same problems and made them complicated. They were forever suggesting that a problem might stem from childhood and be involved with feelings toward a mother or father. All this was often convincing—that was the trouble. It made the commercial seem fraudulent.

—Erik Barnouw

Caution! Television Watching May Be Hazardous to Your Mental Health

Television not only distributes programs and sells products, it also preaches a general philosophy of life. Television tells us, hour after gruesome hour, that the primary measure of an individual's worth is his consumption of products, his measuring up to ideals that are found in packages mass produced and distributed by corporate America. Many products (and even programs), but especially the drug commercials, sell the gospel that there are instant solutions to life's most pressing personal problems. You don't need to think about your own emotional maturity and development of individuality; about discipline, training, and education; about your perception of the world; about your willingness to cooperate and compromise and work with other people; or about developing deep and meaningful human relationships and trying to keep them in repair. "Better living through chemistry" is not just DuPont's slogan. It's one of the commandments of consumerism.

Television—which Professor Galbraith has characterized as one of the "prime instruments for the manipulation of consumer demand"—educates us away from life and away from our individuality. It drives us to line up at the counters of drugstores and supermarkets, shaping our needs and wants, and ultimately ourselves, into the molds that are the products. Not only do the programs and commercials explicitly preach materialism, conspicuous consumption, status consciousness, sexploitation, and fantasy worlds of quick shallow solutions, but even the settings and subliminal messages are commercials for the consumption style of life.

MAN: Man, it's a bug the way that guy got on my back today.

WOMAN: Sam.

MAN: Wrong figures, bring the other file. Come on with that report.

WOMAN: Sam, I've never seen you like this.

MAN: Oh, he's driving me nuts with that big deal. We got any aspirin?

WOMAN: You got a headache?

MAN: Who said anything about a headache. I'm just tense, nervous. I—

WOMAN: Aspirin's for minor pain or headache.

MAN: What do I want, Compoz?

WOMAN: That's just what you want. Compoz, that little gentle blue pill Compoz.

> —a television commercial

WOMAN 1: Here you are, dear.

WOMAN 2: Oh thanks, but I can't look at another dress. All this shopping has given me such a headache.

WOMAN 1: I'll get you something.

WOMAN 2: Wait a minute, it better be something strong.

WOMAN 1: I've got what you need, Laura.

WOMAN 2: What's that?

WOMAN 1: Anacin.

> —a television commercial

ANNOUNCER: Leave your feeling of tension behind and step into a quiet world. You'll feel calmer, more relaxed with Quiet World.

> —a television commercial

Even though we know we are being taken, we are being taken.

> —William F. Fore

The headache remedy commercials are among the most revealing. A headache is often our body's way of telling us something's wrong. What is wrong may have to do with the bad vibes one picks up working in big corporations' office buildings, or shopping in their stores. The best answer may be to stay out of such places. Obviously, such a solution would be as bad for the corporate state generally as for the headache remedy business in particular. So the message is clear: Corporate jobs and shopping trips are as American as chemical additives in apple pie. You just keep driving yourself through both. And when those mysterious headache devils appear for no reason at all, you swallow the magic chemicals.

But what's true of the magic chemical ads is true of commercials and programs generally. Look at the settings. Auto ads push clothes, fashion, and vacations. Furniture-wax ads push wall-to-wall carpeting and draperies. Breakfast-cereal ads push new stoves and refrigerators. Not surprisingly, the programs do the same—after all, they're paid for by the same guys who pay for the commercials. Dean Martin probably sold as many cigarettes just by smoking them on camera as the Marlboro Man did by riding his horse. How many blacks have commented on the misleading black life style depicted by television shows like *Julia*? Erik Barnouw's three-volume history of broadcasting reveals that the disappearance of the early 1950's dramatists from television was due to advertisers' revulsion at the dramatists' message that happiness could be found by ordinary people in lower-class settings.

You may be saying about this point, "Look, I really do like nightclubs, fast cars, cigarettes, motel

It is the general policy of advertisers to glamorize their products, the people who buy them, and the whole American social and economic scene. . . . The American consuming public as presented by the advertising industry today is middle class, not lower class; happy in general, not miserable and frustrated. . . .

> —a letter from an advertising
> agency explaining rejection of
> Pulitzer Prize-winning play

The tendency [of the mass media] to blunt reason has a more sinister effect than merely selling things to people that they don't want to buy. It also obscures the individual's recognition that the whole system tends to repress his freedom by limiting his real choices and by invading the inner space where he maintains his own sense of personal identity and integrity.

> —William F. Fore

On teevee
    see the looters run
With whiskey
    and cartons
        of cigarettes,
With wigs
    and sofas
        and teevee sets—
Running
    after
        the merchandise
All the
    commercials
        advertise
            on teevee
            on teevee
            on teevee

> —Eve Merriam

decor, and hairspray. If you don't that's your problem. Go live in the woods. But don't hassle me."

I would be the first to acknowledge that we are, of course, talking about matters of personal taste. But two facts remain: (1) The wholly disproportionate—if not exclusive—emphasis of television is pushing only one point of view. The choice you'll never know is the choice you'll never make. Many Americans are not sufficiently informed of the alternatives to make an intelligent choice of the life they most want. (2) Independent students of our society—quite aside from their personal values—believe there is a correlation between the philosophy preached by television and many of our worst social problems.

One of the most vicious of television's predatory habits is its stalking of the poor. The affluent have nothing to lose but their money and control over their own lives and personalities. The poor are not so lucky. They must sit there, without even the liberating knowledge that money can't buy happiness, and constantly be told that their lack of material possessions is a badge of social ostracism in a nation that puts higher stress on monetary values than moral values. Occasionally this frustration breaks out in violence on the streets. Then, for an evening or two, we get a distorted picture of what the problem is, as television brings us the news—followed by another evening of series shows and commercial messages urging conspicuous consumption as the mark of success in life.

Television is really providing no better service, no more responsible programming, for middle-class, adult white males than for anyone else in our society—retired people, minority group members, blue-collar

As a father of four, I have seen the effect of television in the home and in the supermarket. Its impact is felt equally in the nation's public life. And the only thing that surprises me is that there are still some who greet this obvious fact with surprise.

—Robert H. Finch

It takes time, yes, but if you expect to be in business for any length of time, think of what it can mean to your firm in profits if you can condition a million or ten million children who will grow up into adults trained to buy your product as soldiers are trained to advance when they hear the trigger words "forward march."

—Clyde Miller

A study was made of the use of deception in TV comedy. . . . Approximately 25 percent of the situations . . . involved deception as a major or minor part of the plot. Since most of these situation comedies pitch their shows toward children, we might reasonably ask what effect such a large amount of deception has on their values. . . . The correlation between not getting caught on TV and not getting caught cheating in an exam or on an expense account is only open to conjecture.

—William F. Fore

It [TV] leads not toward human interaction, but rather toward withdrawal into private communication with the picture tube and the private life of fantasy. It is aimed less often at solving the problems of life than escaping from them. It is essentially a passive behavior—something a child surrenders himself to, something that is done to and for him, something that he doesn't have to work for or think about or pay for.

—Wilbur Schramm

workers, and so forth. But there are two groups of Americans who are entitled to special mention: children and women.

I begin with children because we can fairly assume, I think, that if television shows little respect for our children it will show even less for the rest of us.

It is shocking enough that we should have to wait until 1969 to get the equivalent of a *Sesame Street*, and that it should then have to come from the impoverished Public Broadcasting System rather than the commercial networks. But even worse than that is the networks' commercial view of our youngsters: They are perceived principally as little consumers, both in their own right and as an additional way of reaching Mom and Dad. Advertisers are quite open about the commercial desirability of hooking consumers young, and they do just that. The networks cooperate—through their National Association of Broadcasters Code of Good Practice—by permitting themselves to show almost twice as many commercials per hour during the Saturday morning children's programs as during the Saturday evening entertainment shows.

Television could be a challenging experience for the young people of our nation during those early formative years. It could help them to learn to grow as human beings, to better understand themselves and the world they are entering. Instead, it encourages our children to continue an infantile withdrawal from the world and a dependence on fantasy. Above all, it encourages them to adopt the hedonistic, conspicuous consumption attitudes and values of their corporate elders.

Women have been telling very well the story of

You use our bodies to sell products! You blackmail us
with the fear of being unloved if we do not buy!

—Marian Delgado

ANNOUNCER: Cigarettes are like women. The best ones are
thin and rich. Silva Thins are thin and rich. Thin so
they taste light, lighter than other 100's, lighter than
most kings. Rich, well because rich is better. Cigarettes
are like women, the best ones are thin and rich. Silva
Thins are thin and rich.

—a television commercial

Many of us break our backs trying to realize the dream,
the synthesis of housewife-sexmate. Many of us fall along
the way, victims of nervous breakdowns, schizophrenia and
sheer exhaustion. But few realize the oppression of the system which propels them unrelentingly towards rotten goals.

—Donna Keck

their portrayal on television. There's really very little I can add. Just as the more sophisticated black commentators describe the role of blacks in America as "the white problem," I believe that the woman's role portrayed on television is creating at least as many problems for men as for women.

If men and women are going to relate to each other as people, neither can perceive the other as an object to be manipulated for purposes of self-gratification. Men and women can help each other to self-realization. Men are robbed of this opportunity equally with women when they are sold an image of women as something less than human and an image of themselves that constantly imposes the need to role-play their masculinity (while simultaneously purchasing seven hundred million dollars worth of cosmetics every year).

Psychiatrists, and others far more knowledgeable than I, believe there may well be some correlation between the television image of women and the problems of· many of suburbia's unhappy housewives: divorce, exhaustion, alcoholism, promiscuity, frustration, anxiety, and mental illness. At the very least, we are not helping our children to develop satisfying attitudes about their sexuality by what we are teaching them in the television commercials.

The image of women in the ... [television series] is *dreadful*. At one pole there's the *I Love Lucy* stereotype, the brainless featherhead, and the sweet, dumb lovable blonde of *Petticoat Junction* and *Green Acres* who's helpless without men. In between, there's the maternal nurturing housewife, like Donna Reed or Julia—passive women who are defined in terms of their relationship to men—as wives or mothers or widows. At the other pole there's the male fantasy of the "liberated" woman—the chic, hard, cold, sexy swinger with no ties, who obviously sleeps around and is not an economic drag on the man. And there's nothing else. It has almost no relationship with reality at all.

—Robin Morgan

One can search television for a long time before finding a mature sexual relationship.

—Norman Mark

What aspects of being a man or woman in today's world could be useful in advertising a product, other than the erotic? Strength of character? Shouldering responsibility? Compassion? Service? Practicing a profession?

—Mary S. Calderone

There is such a thing as psychological suicide in which one does not take his own life by a given act, but dies because he has chosen—perhaps without being entirely aware of it—not to live.

—Rollo May

Sex

Big business has even prostituted
Sex
By using it to sell
In greed
Publicly
Making it more difficult
For the rest of us
To use properly
For giving
In love
Privately

It could be otherwise. I, for one, do not believe the economy would suffer one bit if television were to portray men and women in healthy relationships as mature people. However, even if such honesty would hurt the sales of some products, such a reform would seem to me to be worth almost any price we might pay.

Finally, if it is true that passivity and a sense of powerlessness are among the most dangerous epidemics in our society today, the television set is suspect at the outset regardless of what's programmed on it. It is so busy getting us to turn *it* on that it educates us away from life. It makes an affirmative effort to deaden our senses. It encourages us to depend on it like a drug—with comparable effects reported by doctors. It comforts us and says it's all right for us to return to the womb of its warm glow. It is a communication medium that discourages, and makes more difficult, communication and a sense of community among Americans. It gives us a fantasy world, presented as reality, that is almost diabolically constructed to increase, rather than decrease, mental illness, frustration, anxiety, and despair when, on those rare occasions, we leave our tele-

Owen Jennison [had died from starvation]. . . . A small black cylinder protruded from the top of his head. . . .

It was a standard surgical job. . . . I touched the ecstasy plug with my . . . fingertips, then ran them down the hair-fine wire going deep into Owen's brain, down into the pleasure center.

No, the extra current hadn't killed him. What had killed Owen was his lack of will power. He had been unwilling to get up.

—Larry Niven, a science fiction short story

When I'm drivin' in my car,
And that man comes on the radio;
And he's tellin' me more and more
About some useless information,
Supposed to fire my imagination?
I can't get no satisfaction.

When I'm watchin' my T. V.,
And that man comes on to tell me
How white my shirts can be,
I can't get no satisfaction.

—Mick Jagger and Keith Richard

vision sets and venture out into that other world.

The only exceptions would be programs like Jack LaLanne's exercises, or Public Broadcasting's offerings of Laura Weber's guitar lessons and Julia Child's cooking programs. Television could urge us to get up, turn off the set, and go live a little. It might even say, "We interrupt this program to bring you a special announcement. The sun is now setting. It's a much more beautiful sight than anything we can offer. We urge you to get up and go outdoors and watch it. We will temporarily suspend broadcasting until dark." Television could help us to lead more interesting, more informed, more fulfilling lives. With rare exceptions, it does not.

The true business of people should be to . . . think about whatever it was they were thinking about before somebody came along and told them they had to earn a living.

—Buckminster Fuller

We've got to get ourselves back to the garden.

—Joni Mitchell

When I was a kid, I figured like everyone else does that the more money I had, the more things I'd possess and the happier I'd be. Well, I was lucky. I obtained the material things when I was relatively young. And it didn't take long to figure out what a ridiculous goal that was.

—Glenn Yarbrough

I wanted to live deep and suck out all the marrow of life, to live so sturdily and Spartan-like as to put to rout all that was not life, to cut a broad swath and shave close, to drive life into a corner, and reduce it to its lowest terms, and, if it proved to be mean, why then to get the whole and genuine meanness of it, and publish its meanness to the world; or if it were sublime, to know it by experience, and be able to give a true account of it in my next excursion.

—Henry David Thoreau

"Okay, what's the alternative?" you ask.

How about life? How about trying to find out what you would do, and be, and think, and create if there wasn't some corporation trying to sell you on doing it all their way?

But how would you go about that?

It soon became obvious that if I was going to criticize television for not offering alternative life styles, I was going to have to be able to find the answer to that question. So I set about it.

I think experience is useful to understanding. When I was trying to understand the problems of creative artists in television, I got an 8-mm camera and tried to make some films; I tried writing some poetry and songs and playing the guitar. When the FCC was involved in evaluating questions of journalistic freedom, I watched and talked to the radio and television reporters themselves as well as listening to the formal presentations of their lawyers.

As with any inquiry, a search for alternative life styles can best be begun by identifying, segregating, examining, and experiencing the most basic components of the subject. In this case, the subject was life. Whether or not you permanently leave the city to live in the woods, a natural environment is a good place to sort out the basics of living. I have always enjoyed hiking and camping anyway, and the West Virginia mountains seemed the best setting for my new odyssey.

For two weeks in August, 1970, my boys—Sherman, age nine, and Gregory, age six—and I lived on some isolated forested land in the mountains of West Virginia. The only radio station we could hear was WELD in Fisher, West Virginia—a town about ten

And now a man came up and asked him, "Master, what good must I do to gain eternal life?" "Good?" said Jesus. "Why do you ask me about that? One alone is good. But if you wish to enter into life, keep the commandments." ... The young man answered, "I have kept all these. Where do I still fall short?" Jesus said to him, "If you wish to go the whole way, go, sell your possessions, and give to the poor, and then you will have riches in heaven; and come, follow me." When the young man heard this, he went away with a heavy heart; for he was a man of great wealth.

—Matthew 19:16–22

Economically the successes achieved in the working out of the Vermont project far outweighed the failures. First and foremost, our idea of a subsistence homestead economy proved easy of realization. In exchange for a few months per year of carefully planned bread labor, we were able to provide ourselves with the bulk of our year's food. A few weeks of work furnished our house fuel. Another few weeks provided the needed repairs and replacements on buildings, tools and equipment.

—Helen and Scott Nearing

miles away with a population of twenty-five or thirty. Bordering the town was the somewhat larger community of Moorefield, where we did our shopping. But we were five miles down a state highway from Moorefield and another five miles up a barely passable rocky mountain road that forded a stream twenty times on its way to our wilderness campsite. So we were pretty much on our own.

Because we had never owned much in the way of elaborate camping gear, because it had been a while since we had done this kind of camping, and because I have never really been leisurely or organized enough to plan carefully what I am going to take, we wound up starting life from scratch in a number of respects. For example, we began getting water by dipping tin cups into the stream and pouring the water into an old gallon milk container. One day I saw a washbasin and bucket in the Moorefield hardware store and suddenly realized the washbasin could be used for dipping water much more efficiently into the bucket. It was almost as if I had invented both objects then and there.

We did a lot of our own food gathering (including the discovery of friendly and generous Farmer Mathias on the top of our mountain), cooking, washing, minor mending, health care, and fire building. We also constructed a very grand outhouse as a tangible token of our appreciation to our friends, Susan and Jerry Inman, whose land it was. We walked through the mountains and played in the streams and watched the sky and talked a lot. I also took the time to relax, and think, and write in a journal—especially at night, when the moon was full and my boys were asleep.

Out of this West Virginia experience came a num-

When we depend less on industrially produced consumer goods, we can live in quiet places. Our bodies become vigorous; we discover the serenity of living with the rhythms of the earth. We cease oppressing one another.

—Alicia Bay Laurel

Biologically, each member of the human family posses-ses inborn differences based on his brain structure and on his vast mosaic of endocrine glands—in fact, on every aspect of his physical being. Each of us has a distinctive set of drives—for physical activity, for food, for sexual expression, for power. Each one has his own mind quali-ties: abilities, ways of thinking, and patterns of mental conditions. Each one has his own emotional setup and his leanings toward music and art in its various forms, includ-ing literature. All these leanings are subject to change and development, but there is certainly no mass movement toward uniformity. No one ever "recovers" from the fact that he was born an individual.

—Roger J. Williams

For my panacea ... let me
have a draught of undiluted
morning air.

—Henry David Thoreau

ber of significant insights for me. I'll try to explain the philosophy that emerged, and why I think it came out of that setting.

I don't think it's enough simply to tell someone: "Be yourself." It's not bad as a two-word philosophy, but it's not much help as a guide. In order to be yourself you have to be by yourself. And I don't mean simply alone. You can't be alone in a big city; there's your car, and the architecture, and the radio and television, and your clothes, and the packaged foods—all that stuff that keeps getting in the way of whatever you might be if it weren't there.

To be by yourself you have to experience, at least briefly and as closely as is possible, the conditions under which you would have lived two thousand, or twenty thousand, years ago. You started there, because the history of man, as most of us think of it, started there. And you are, among other things, the embodiment of man—the current end product of human evolution. If you are ever to understand where you're at, you have to know where you began.

Try to think through and meditate on your thousands of years of civilization. For most of those years you will live a nomadic or agrarian existence. What are the first things you need, I mean *really* need? Love? Air? Water? Food? Clothing? Shelter? In about that order? At what point in your development will you try to fashion utensils or furniture of some kind out of wood or stone? When do you start a garden? When will you domesticate animals for their milk or meat or transportation? In what ways do you start bringing aesthetic pleasure into your life—an artistic touch to an object, or a little music? Do you develop a religion?

Every little boy ought to hear the bluebirds
    singing in the early autumn
Look up and see the grey goose winging
         • • •
But how you gonna hear a bluebird in
    a noisy old town
How you gonna see a grey goose with all
    the smog, fog and smoke
      Keep the goose from coming around
         • • •
How you gonna dig in the sidewalks of a
    dirty dirty town
How you gonna fish in a babbling brook
    when there ain't nothing but cement
    around
How you gonna hear a bluebird when all
    you hear is noisy cars, trucks and buses
    going round.

—R. Self
"What Every Little Boy Ought to Know," by R. Self.

To be totally intelligent would be
to be half stupid, you've got
to feel half of it to see
if it's any good.

—Mason Williams

In regard to the inorganic universe, I see our relation
rather like that of a sculptor. No sculptor whom I have ever
spoken to thinks of enforcing his forms on nature. He thinks:
"I lay bare, I realize in stone, a form that is latently there."

—W. H. Auden

My boys and I didn't set out to go through this experience; it just kind of evolved as I thought about it. Actually, I think it would be a worthwhile thing to try to structure in modest ways and use as an educational experience for a high-school or college class— or curriculum. We had brought some objects with us, which we used—such as the tin cup and gallon milk container I mentioned. But seeing the pail and washbowl was as if I'd invented them myself, and the experience provided an insight into what it must be like for people at any time to see the relationship between newly discovered objects and a problem at hand. We dug a small pit for waste dishwater, not because we'd read the Boy Scout manual, but because the campsite was beginning to get a little muddy after a couple of days. We piled up stones to sit on because it was more comfortable than sitting on the dirt. The point is, building a life for yourself in this trial-and-error, learning-by-experience fashion gives you a much greater sense of self than simply moving into a fully equipped suburban house, accepting what's there, and buying what's not after a television commercial has urged you to do so.

As a record along the way, I write in a journal. My journal is bound, so that I'll take it more seriously and won't lose the pages. (I formerly jotted notes on sheets of yellow pads.) It's not a diary. It's a sketchbook: furniture designs, speech drafts, silly thoughts, serious reflections, and drawings, all mixed together as life is—or should be. It's my personal equivalent of mankind's museums and libraries. It's a tangible record of the balance in my life. It makes me see better and take life with both more seriousness and more whimsey. I like it.

Draw near to Nature.... Try, like some first human being, to say what you see and experience and love and lose. . . . Seek those [themes] which your own everyday life offers you; describe your sorrows and desires, passing thoughts and the belief in some sort of beauty—describe all these with loving, quiet, humble sincerity, and use, to express yourself, the things in your environment, the images from your dreams, and the objects of your memory.

—Rainer Maria Rilke

I'm livin' a life I can't slow down, 'cept with a
    song.
And I wanna know how the people made it
    without big corporations,
And I wanna feel how the people lived when
    life was slow.

—Margaret Lewis and Mira Smith

We simply propose that our social and economic ideal be *that society which gives the maximum opportunity for each person in it to realize himself, to develop and use his potentialities and to labor as a human being of dignity giving to and receiving from his fellow men.*

—Rollo May

The man who . . . abandons all pride
of possession . . . reaches the goal of peace
supreme.

—Bhagavad Gita

If you are to personally experience the process of civilization it can't be by a fill-in-the-dots approach. You don't just do the equivalent of going into the chemistry lab and following what the lab manual says, step-by-step. That's what's wrong with most cookbooks, in my judgment. They tell you how to make a given dish—exactly. If you're lucky you can repeat the recipe later and the same thing will happen. But you don't know why or how it happened, or the process by which the originator came up with that combination, or how you might come up with something similarly delightful. (I generally read all the recipes utilizing the ingredients I have at hand and then do my own thing— being careful to record precisely what I am doing in my journal in case it accidentally turns out to be edible.)

So you start asking yourself with some regularity, "Why am I doing it this way?" "Do I really need this particular object in my life?" Once you have been through this process you *can* be yourself. You know who you are and why you have selected each of your possessions. You have internalized the history of civilization; you know the reasons for what you do and why you do it—not just intellectually, but within the core of your soul and the marrow of your bones. They are your reasons, worked out of your life, and recorded in your book.

Prior to my West Virginia experience most of my professional life had been just that, a professional life—using such skills as I picked up along the way to do the kinds of things that lawyers, professors, and public officials do. That's an important part of life, I think. Most grown men and women need to have the

I've got everything a man could ever need
I've got dreams to dream and songs to sing in
    the morning
I've got hands to hold my baby child and eyes to
    watch my woman smile
I've got everything a man could ever need

—Mac Davis

I must help myself out from twilight and sleep ... exert
myself to arouse and shape half-grown and half-dead facilities in myself, if I am not in the end to escape into a sad
resignation. ...

—Holderlin

Much unhappiness and many suicides can be traced
to misguided desire to be something other than one's self.
Each of us as an individual has the problem of finding his
way through life as best he can. Knowing one's self as a
distinctive individual should be an important goal of education; it will help pave the road each of us travels in his
pursuit of happiness.

—Roger J. Williams

For one human being to love another: that is perhaps
the most difficult of all our tasks, the ultimate, the last
test and proof, the work for which all other work is but
preparation.

—Rainer Maria Rilke

Money can't buy love, money can't
    buy love
It can buy a whole lot of stuff but money
    can't buy love

—Betty Craig

sense that they are capable of, and are involved in, productivity that is paid for or otherwise generally recognized as valuable to society. The problem, of course, is that it is too easy for such activities to consume virtually all of your intellectual, emotional, and physical energy—as they had for me.

As I thought about the other basic elements of life, I began by asking, "If I were to plan an ideal day, what would it contain?"

Most fundamental, I suppose, is love. Each of us has had different feelings and relationships we have thought of as love. Sexuality can be an important part of it. Each of us means something a little different by it. But we would probably all agree that love is a great deal more than adulation or infatuation, a temporary soporific for loneliness, or lust.

To love another, to share, to want to give of oneself, to simultaneously study and experience life, another person, yourself, and a relationship, is surely one of the most exhilarating, volatile, and satisfying of human conditions.

There's very little more I should or need contribute to the thousands of volumes, poems, and songs on that subject.

Contemplation of some kind has been considered fundamental by man throughout the ages. I decided to include it as another basic element. It can be religion, philosophy, mythology, yoga, or whatever makes sense for you. But we have to have some time when we think beyond our hangnails and hangovers and the daily routine to a somewhat more meaningful view of life.

Boy: If I use Listerine every day I get the girl, right?
Friend: Unless she gets you first.
Boy: Yeah, right.

—a television commercial

People who talk about "America's spiritual crisis" see TV as a symbol.

—Staughton Lynd

But no matter how much one discounts the failures of religion, he must in the end come back to the moral teachers for the guidance needed. The United States at this time does not require a new church; it does require the insights which Judaism, Christianity, Islam and Buddhism have nurtured, and it is from such insights that the new spiritual agreement will evolve.

—James A. Michener

A mediocre person moderately gifted . . . exercising the gift in his own sincere and humble way . . . is *ipso facto* a more cultured individual than a person of brilliant endowments who has acquainted himself in a general way with all the "best" that has been thought and felt and done, but who has never succeeded in bringing any portion of his range of interests into direct relation with his volitional self, with the innermost shrine of his personality.

—Edward A. Sapir

Personal analysis is a related activity. Psychiatrists or counseling services or encounter groups are one way to do it. But thinking, writing in a journal, or regularly talking with a trusted friend are other ways to achieve related benefits. Most of us could do with a little more knowledge about why we tick the way we do.

Creative expression is especially important. The opportunity to be creative—personally, not professionally—as well as to be exposed to beauty and the best creativity of others, is essential to individual growth. This is one of television's greatest sins. It fails to expose us to the best that man has to offer. It says, "Television and artistic creativity are for professionals like us. They are not something you should even dream of doing for yourself." It almost never shows us how we can experience our own artistic creativity in our daily lives. And it renders us passive during time we could be spending in personal growth.

Regular contact with nature is a necessary reminder of the whole earth system from which we came, in which we live, and to which we will return. Living in the woods may or may not be the best way to keep in touch with our origins. But it is a decidedly impractical way for that 90 percent of the American people who live in cities. I considered, and fairly quickly rejected, the thought of commuting to Washington from West Virginia. But I have made a special effort to live near a park or wilderness area with which I can have daily contact, to plant flowers and vegetables outside my apartment windows, and to keep some bird feeders filled. You can keep plants in your home and office. Have a picnic lunch in a downtown park. Look at the sky. Walk in the rain.

I am sorry
For the men of these times. They
Talk of nothing interesting
And have no ambition and
Die without ever being
Aware of the music of verse

—Ou Yang Hsiu

We have fallen out of nature and hang suspended in space.

—Hermann Hesse

One would think from the talk of men that riches and poverty were a great matter; and our civilization mainly respects it. But the Indians say that they do not think the white man, with his brow of care, always toiling, afraid of heat and cold, and keeping within doors, has any advantage of them. The permanent interest of every man is never to be in a false position, but to have the weight of Nature to back him in all that he does.

—Ralph Waldo Emerson

Most of the luxuries, and many of the so-called comforts of life, are not only not indispensable, but positive hindrances to the elevation of mankind.

—Henry David Thoreau

The perfect Sage . . . is content to give up extravagant comforts . . . and thus to set the nation an example of returning to simplicity.

—The Book of Tao

Camping in the mountains for two weeks also reaffirmed my latent but basic commitment to the psychic values of simplicity. You not only can get along with substantially fewer "things" when camping in the woods, but you actually enjoy life more because it is not so cluttered with objects. The experience gave me a way of thinking about simplicity, objects, and natural living that I had not had before. And it impressed upon me, for perhaps the first time, a sense of the interrelated totality of "life-support activities"—another basic element of life.

By life-support activities I mean the provision of those things that are necessary to sustain our physical life: food, clothing, shelter, transportation, and so forth. These are the kinds of activities that I became most fully aware of in the woods because I had to, and because they can be most easily comprehended when reduced to basics.

In an industrialized urban environment, it is easy to forget that human life still is, as it was originally, sustained by certain basic functions. I think some participation in the support of your life is essential to a sense of fulfillment. And yet, I used to give almost no attention to these kinds of activities. Food simply appeared on my dinner table ready to be eaten. The house I lived in was purchased, not built by me. It was warmed or cooled by some equipment in the basement that I knew very little about and was tended to by repairmen when necessary. Clothing was something I found in closets and dresser drawers and was cleaned and mended by my wife, the maid, or a cleaning establishment. Transportation was provided by the municipal bus system for commuting and by FCC drivers during

The Indian's salmon-spearing is a culturally higher type of activity than that of the telephone girl or mill hand simply because there is normally no sense of spiritual frustration during its prosecution, no feeling of subservience to tyrannous yet largely inchoate demands, because it works in naturally with all the rest of the Indian's activities instead of standing out as a desert patch of merely economic effort in the whole of life.

—Edward A. Sapir

With no intermediaries, such as supermarkets and banks, there is a direct relationship between work and survival. It is thus possible for even the most repetitive jobs such as washing dishes or sawing wood to be spiritually rewarding.

—Sara Davidson

A specter is stalking in our midst whom only a few see with clarity. It is not the old ghost of communism or fascism. It is a new specter: a completely mechanized society, devoted to maximal material output and consumption, directed by computers; and in this social process, man himself is being transformed into a part of the total machine, well fed and entertained, yet passive, unalive, and with little feeling.

—Erich Fromm

When art becomes inseparable from daily living—the way a woman prepares a meal, speaks to her children, decorates her home, makes love, laughs—there is no "art," for all life is artistic.

—Edmund Carpenter

the day. At my office, I was surrounded not only by machines—copying machines, electric typewriters, dictating machines—but also by people paid to operate them for me, answer my telephone, and bring me coffee.

In short, I had taken very nearly all of my life-support activities—my life—and cut them up into bits and pieces that I parceled out to individuals, corporations, and machines around me. This was extraordinarily efficient in one sense; that is, I was working at perhaps 98 percent of the level of professional production of which I am capable. But I concluded that it was bad for life, for I was living only a small percentage of my ultimate capacity to live.

A number of things happen to us when we avoid participation in our life-support activities: we get less physical activity than we need, we tend to detach ourselves psychologically from the real world, and we begin to internalize our society's prejudice that thinkers and administrators are engaged in a higher form of enterprise than others. This is bound to affect the traditional relationship between a husband and wife, and it has provided bitter fuel to the current women's movement.

Consider this scene. The husband comes home, kisses his wife, tells her now nice she looks, accepts a drink from her, and begins sharing the events of the day: the deals he's closed, the important people he's talked or lunched with, the papers he's published, the television show he's done, or what not. He then reads the evening paper while the meal is put on the table, eats with the family, compliments his wife on the dinner, retires to watch television or do some more paper

Capitol Punishment

The Great
TV Blackout

By Art Buchwald

A week ago Sunday, New York City had a blackout which caused all nine television stations in the area to go out for several hours. This created tremendous crises in families all over the New York area, and proved that TV plays a much greater role in people's lives than anyone can imagine.

For example, when the TV went off in the Bufkins' house in Forest Hills, Long Island, panic set in. First, Bufkins thought it was his set in the living room, so he rushed into his bedroom and turned on that set: Nothing.

The phone rang and Mrs. Bufkins heard her sister in Manhattan tell her that there was a blackout.

She hung up and said to her husband, "It isn't your set. Something's happened to the top of the Empire State building."

Bufkins stopped and said, "Who are you?"

"I'm your wife, Edith."

"Oh," Bufkins said. "Then I suppose those kids in there are mine."

"That's right," Mrs. Bufkins said. "If you ever got out of that armchair in front of the TV set, you'd know who we were."

"Boy, they've really grown," Bufkins said, looking at his son and daughter. "How old are they now?"

"Thirteen and fourteen," Mrs. Bufkins replied.

"I'll be darned. Hi, kids."

"Who's he?" Bufkins' son Henry asked.

"It's your father," Mrs. Bufkins said.

work, and comes out long enough to read the children a story before bed. An idyllic scene? Admittedly it's better than most. But look at what the husband is saying to his wife (and children) *by his actions*: physical exertion and life-support activities are not something he values, or considers worthy of his participation. He cannot comprehend what is involved in such activities; his appreciation (if his verbiage comes through as sincere at all) is obviously for something very peripheral to his consciousness, his values, and his life.

In fact, actual participation in life-support activities is not even enough—by itself. Take the husband who helps out around the house—perhaps with some of the heavy cleaning or by occasionally doing the dishes. Notice the different attitudes he can bring to it: (1) He can do it begrudgingly, complaining all the time. If so, his work is not likely to be of very good quality— and besides, who needs it? (2) He can do it absentmindedly; he doesn't complain (even under his breath), but he's not really into it either. (3) Or he can do it in order to be fair ("We both share the work around our house."). Even this husband, I would contend, is missing the point—and contributing to unnecessary distance between himself and his wife and his life. For he is still saying, by his words and his actions, that the work he is doing is something in the nature of a nuisance that must be removed, a temporary interruption in an otherwise pleasant day. His joy, his fulfillment, his worth as a human being, continue to come from what he does at the office or by way of hobbies.

Once a husband and wife begin to share a common appreciation of the physical, psychological, and spiritual values of participating in their own life-support activi-

"I'm pleased to meetcha," Bufkins' daughter Mary said shyly.

There was an embarrassed silence all around.

"Look," said Bufkins finally. "I know I haven't been much of a father, but now that the TV's out I'd like to make it up to you."

"How?" asked Henry.

"Well, let's just talk," Bufkins said. "That's the best way to get to know each other."

"What do you want to talk about?" Mary asked.

"Well, for starters, what school do you go to?"

"We go to Forest Hills high school," Henry said.

"What do you know?" Bufkins said. "You're both in high school."

There was a dead silence.

"What do *you* do?" Mary asked.

"I'm an accountant," Bufkins said.

"I thought you were a car salesman," Mrs. Bufkins said in surprise.

"That was two years ago. Didn't I tell you I changed jobs?" Bufkins said.

"No, you didn't. You haven't told me anything for two years."

"Yup. I'm doing quite well too," Bufkins said.

"Then why am I working in a department store?" Mrs. Bufkins demanded.

"Oh, are you still working in a department store? If I had known that, I would have told you you could quit last year. You should have mentioned it," Bufkins said.

There was more dead silence.

Finally Henry said, "Hey, you want to hear me play the guitar?"

"I'll be darned. You know how to play the guitar? Say, didn't I have a daughter who played the guitar?"

"That was Susie," Mrs. Bufkins said.

ties, they have entered into a new dimension of their lives—as individuals and as a couple. They do not even need to do the same things. A husband who keeps the garage in a semblance of order can recognize a tidy kitchen when he sees one; and when he compliments his wife on the fact, it conveys much more than when the same words are genuinely spoken by a man who never lifts a finger around the house. If a man has tended the garden, he can appreciate the jars of fruits and vegetables—canned by his wife—with a depth of understanding otherwise impossible. If he has worked in leather he can more fully appreciate what she has sewn from cloth.

The central criterion is a committed participation in life-support activities growing out of a recognition of their essential contribution to a full and happy human life. If a husband can truly internalize these attitudes, he will be more fulfilled as a whole person in a society that is increasingly emphasizing smaller and smaller bits of him as his valuable "specialization." Equally, or more important, he can then communicate to his wife— by his actions—a genuine appreciation of her worth and a participation in her world and her life.

Nor are these shared understandings limited to a husband and wife. If you do your own simple electric wiring around the house, you begin to have a much greater appreciation for the worth of an auto mechanic who has skill and pride in his work. If you type, you begin to develop more appreciation for a secretary who can turn out clean fast copy.

Now I'm not proposing that you do everything for yourself. For one thing, you cannot trace everything back to first elements. You can build your own furni-

"Where is she?"

"She got married a year ago, just about the time you were watching the World Series."

"How about that?" Bufkins said, very pleased. "You know, I hope they don't fix the antenna for another couple hours. There's nothing like a blackout for a man to *really* get to know his family."

—The Washington Post
Copyright 1971 by Art Buchwald

Eskimo, for example, don't put art into their environment: they treat the environment itself as art form.

Life-as-art is taken for granted by preliterate peoples, many of whom have no word for "art." Among the Naskapi, hunting is a holy occupation in which artists engage. Sioux walk-in-a-sacred-manner when on a buffalo hunt. The Balinese say, "We like to do all things beautifully."

—Edmund Carpenter

I wanted to live somewhere where I could hike and hunt. ... I had five small children growing up next to a big sinful city. I didn't really like labor relations. ... I've met wonderful people here who hold very simple, unimportant jobs. I got a little arrogant when I was at United.

—a former United Air Lines labor relations executive

Lives based on having are less free than lives based either on doing or on being.

—William James

ture. But are you going to saw your own boards from your own trees? Must you make your own nails? Even the most deeply committed do-it-yourselfers reach some accommodation with civilization.

In the second place, you simply don't have time to do it all. To raise and can all your own fruits and vegetables, for example, would take substantially more time per year than most people are prepared to give to it—especially if you are also personally constructing your own house, weaving your own material, making your own clothes, and walking everywhere.

In the third place, there are a lot of conveniences of urbanized life that are there anyway that you might as well use. They can save you time you might rather spend in more satisfying ways. There's no point in cooking in your fireplace every night—or on your corporate cookout charcoal grill—if you have a gas or electric range sitting in your kitchen.

But you can try to do a little bit of all your life-support activities and a substantial amount of whichever one or two of them appeal to you and make the most practical sense for you. I have taken to tending a simple garden, preparing my own simple foods, doing some modest mending of clothes, and providing my own transportation by bicycle. You can find the activities that fit best into your own life pattern.

Lately it seems,
Everything I see
Tells me life is movin' much too fast
And underneath the strain,
Folks don't act the same
And if that's progress,
I'll take the past

Gonna find myself a country road
With grassy fields on either side
Gonna put on my boots and my jeans and my
    country hat
Gonna sit by a stream as the sun goes down
And straighten out my mind
Gonna soothe my soul
And go back to where it's at

You can have your concrete cities,
You can have your poisoned air
You can have your smoke a rollin' from the stack
And don't offer me your pity,
And don't call me square
Just because I see where things have jumped the track
                                        —Bobby Bond

Try making love without drugs, alcohol, tobacco, television, mechanical music, printed matter, shopping (except for food) or automobile driving, for one month. Or for one week. Or for a day.

                                        —Ann-Elizabeth

Nature . . . becomes to [man] the measure of his attainments. So much of nature as he is ignorant of, so much of his own mind does he not yet possess. And, in fine, the ancient precept, "know thyself," and the modern precept, "study nature," become at last one maxim.
                                        —Ralph Waldo Emerson

This is a "how to" book in the most fundamental sense. If, after reading it, you continue to think about and participate in your life the same as before, the book has failed. It also fails if you simply copy it. The examples I've given—and those that follow—are merely intended as catalysts to your own imagination.

Here's a general principle for a starter. It's what lawyers would call a "rebuttable presumption": unless you can demonstrate why it shouldn't apply, you use it. The presumption is that the best thing (object, process, attitude) for you is the one that man used when he began an agrarian life. There will be, of course, a great many exceptions to this rebuttable presumption. Polio vaccine, so far as I know, has prevented a great deal of human misery with no adverse side effects. I see no reason why its use shouldn't be encouraged even though our first ancestors didn't use it. When I am going from Washington to Los Angeles on business I use airplanes and rented automobiles. "Perma-press" shirts are a godsend; I can get some satisfaction from ironing, I suppose, but I wouldn't cotton to it on a regular basis.

There are also some quite natural activities that are simply forbidden by law or social custom. Running about with brief (or no) clothes may be best for healthy skin, but it's apt to land you in jail. Outhouses may be a form of recycling that will produce fantastic tomatoes, but the law (and the high concentration of urban neighbors) requires that we all use indoor toilets and the corporate sewerage system.

It is not easy to cast aside any culturally ingrained habit or attitude—nor should you, necessarily. The most important thing is to think about what you are

hooray for bakin' soda
ain't it neat
and cheers for
national bakin' soda week
for folks that's young
and folks that's old
bicarbonate of soda
will cure that cold
it cleans your teeth
and prevents the flu
and you can use it
in your car battery too
it puts out fires
of fat or grease
pass the bakin' soda
please

—John Hartford

Do you need these? Explore the following list and decide which of the items on it are essential and which are merely "convenient."

- Electric comb
- Electric knife or carver
- Electric charcoal starter
- Electric can opener
- Electric broiler (besides the broiler in your oven)
- Electric hedge trimmers
- Power lawnmower
- Electric shaver
- Higher intensity lighting
- Home garbage compactor
- Home incinerator
- Total air conditioning
- Food waste disposal unit

There are non-polluting alternatives to each of these that consume less energy and cost less to buy and to operate.

—Paul Swatek

doing, relate it to the early agrarian standard, consider the extent to which some corporation is profiting from your present pattern, ask yourself about alternatives, and wonder whether you might not be more content and fulfilled if you were to change in some minor (or major) way. Let's see how it works.

Start by searching your house or apartment for things you can throw away. Ask yourself, "If I were living in the woods, would I spend a day going to town to buy this aerosol can?" Look for simple substitutes.

Take bicarbonate of soda, for example. You can substitute it for the following products: toothpaste, gargle and mouthwash, burn ointment, bath salts, stomach settlers, room freshener, fire extinguisher, ice-box cleaner, children's clay, and baking powder. And it costs only twenty-seven cents a pound! If a woman feels she simply must use beauty aids other than fresh air, sleep, exercise, proper nutrition, and soap and water, she will find that bulk cold cream is as effective as dozens of cosmetics costing ten to one hundred times as much. When nutrition, exercise, rest, and massage fail you, and a headache remedy is called for, bulk "house-brand" aspirin (at ten cents a hundred) is as effective as highly advertised products costing five to ten times as much.

Look for unnecessary appliances or other machinery. Bread can be toasted in the broiler of the stove. Carving knives really need not be electrically powered. You can put fruit and vegetable waste in a compost heap instead of down an electric disposal. I took up shaving with a blade, brush, and shaving soap instead of with an electric razor. It's kind of bloody, but it's more fun.

Blow up your TV
Throw away your paper
Go to the country
Build you a home
Plant a little garden
Eat a lot of peaches
Try and find Jesus
On your own

—John Prine

MAN: A fine way to wind up your honeymoon! Having
    your bride say, "You have perspiration odor!"
WOMAN: Well, you do, honey.
MAN: I use a deodorant.
WOMAN: You need more. You need my Palmolive Gold!
ANNOUNCER: Palmolive Gold has more hexachlorophene
    to stop odor than any other leading soap.
WOMAN: The honeymoon over?
MAN: Just beginning.
JINGLE: Don't wait to be told you need Palmolive Gold.

—a television commercial

ANNOUNCER: If you like the kind of adventures that befall
    you as a handsome, debonair, swashbuckling young
    rake, you can continue using Great Day [shampoo
    color lotion] after your vacation's over. If you don't
    like looking handsome, debonair, and swashbuckling,
    nothing's lost. You can always go back to looking old.

—a television commercial

Sharpen up your senses. Primitive man had much sharper hearing and sight than you and I. The corporate state wants you to buy its spicy seasoning to put on its bland preprocessed foods, to smell its perfumes and deodorants, to listen to its automobile radios and phonograph records, to look at its ubiquitous commercial announcements—and to feel nothing. Leave it behind. Find some fresh air and breathe deeply. Find some organically grown foods and enjoy the delightful sensation of tasting real fruits and vegetables. Listen to the birds, or the water passing over rocks in a stream. Watch the sun set, or a leaf fall from a tree. Feel the wind upon your skin.

That's the general idea. Now let's take a little more systematic look at our lives with this perspective.

Your body
The corporate state tells you to ignore your body and concentrate on its coverings. You must wear a uniform: a business suit, a cocktail dress, or a regulation tennis outfit, depending on the occasion. We are urged to evaluate ourselves by the standards of *Vogue, Playboy,* and *Esquire.* When we don't measure up, women are urged to buy padded bras, men are encouraged to take a muscle building course, and both are made to feel they must go on crash diets—all at some corporation's profit.

There's nothing wrong in adorning your person in an original fashion that suits your own personality, that gives you the psychological satisfaction of identifying with some group, or that contributes to some ceremonial occasion. I don't particularly dig "fashion" myself, but mankind has for ages. The principal thing to guard against is that you are not simply buying

Hello to the good old summertime! Hello to new romance! Hello to wedding bells that chime! Hello to flirty glances! Goodbye to all those lonely hours I'd spend on Saturday night! No more ignored, now I'm adored, since I switched to Ultra Brite! Ultra Brite toothpaste, a taste you can really feel! Ultra Brite gives your mouth sex appeal!

—a television commercial

WOMAN: I've always heard that men like a good figure. So I—I used Clairol's Great Body. And it—uh—gave my hair a—um—a whole new set of curves. And it— it didn't make my hair feel stiff—feel stiff, either, it just felt like I was wearing a lot of hair. You know, women use Great Body. But it's really for men.

—a television commercial

For fundamentally, drug users are behaving like good American consumers. The mass media tell us continually to satisfy our emotional needs with material products—particularly those involving oral consumption of some kind.

—Philip Slater

cosmetics and clothes in whatever fashions and price ranges the corporations exact from you in exchange for their imprimatur of acceptability.

Recognize the diabolical plot to simultaneously rob and degrade you for what it is, a sick bit of corporate piracy. Reevaluate your standards of physical beauty in yourself and in others. "Diet" to gain health, not to lose weight, unless your overweight is, in fact, a health problem. If you're alone, or with someone who shares your feelings, I'd say the less clothes you wear the better, consistent with warmth, physical protection, and comfort. At the very least, take off your shoes and any undergarments that bind and constrict. Girdles are just designed to get a woman's money and then make her feel uncomfortable—physically and psychologically (she *has* to wear it to be "acceptable," and even then she doesn't make it).

Think about the products you apply to your body. How many do you really want or need, and which ones have been pushed on you by some corporation? We hate to recognize that we have been influenced by commercials; we tend to assume that the four billion dollars spent on radio and television advertising just reaches all those other people. A story is told of a highly educated and proud woman who had just made that point: *She* didn't buy things because of the commercials.

"What toothpaste do you use?" she was asked.

"Gleem," she said during the height of the Gleem commercial campaign a few years ago. ("Gleem is for people who can't brush after every meal.")

"Why?"

"Well," she paused, "I don't know." And then she

Today you're all girl, and being a girl was never nicer. Because this is the age of FDS. FDS was created for a uniquely feminine need. FDS, the first feminine hygiene deodorant spray. Lets you feel as fresh and feminine as you look. Enjoy being a girl. Enjoy a feeling of confidence every day. This is the Age of FDS.

—a television commercial

Seventy years ago, men consumed approximately 6,000 to 6,500 calories daily; women 4,000 to 4,500. Today the average is 2,400 to 2,800 for men and 1,800 to 2,200 for women.

—Adelle Davis

Running opens doors to further thought. It can lead to a new set of values. In itself it's changing your life style.... Just by putting in a physical activity, you're changing your life style, and this may be the first step toward other changes.... Too many people are living sodden, marginal lives. They have just enough energy and interest to raise themselves to a level necessary for life. This is a time to live at the top of your powers. You have to think of yourself as a totality, your body reflects your personality, your mind, your spirit.

—George A. Sheehan

added quickly, "But it's not because of the commercials." Another pause. "It's just, it's just—well, it's just that I can't brush after every meal."

Many of the commercial products are positively harmful to your health, as well as extremely expensive (that advertising's not cheap). A toothpaste advertised to give your mouth sex appeal may cause your teeth to fall out quicker as it dissolves the enamel. The spray from hairspray and deodorants can damage your lungs—and there's certainly no evidence that hairspray does your hair any good, or that perspiration from a healthy body does you any harm. Some doctors have reported that vaginal deodorant spray can cause infection in the tissues for which it is intended and that it's much less effective than soap and water. If you're shaving with a blade razor, a brush and shaving soap (or regular soap) are just as effective (and incredibly cheaper) than an aerosol can of stuff. But ask the more basic question: Why are you shaving at all? As long as it's comfortable, and you get no complaints, what's wrong with a beard or moustache?

Exercise

Early man expended a tremendous amount of physical energy in the course of his daily routine and was in great physical shape as a result. Jogging and sports are all right, but it's more pleasant and natural if you can work your physical exercise into the normal routine of your day: Try walking or bicycling to and from work. Don't pay for some corporate health clubs or golf clubs. Be resentful of corporate America trying to sell you back the health they stole from you. Participation in your life-support activities generally will increase your physical activity. In any event, you and I probably

Another reason why nutritional knowledge is not applied is that much of our information concerning food comes from advertising. Commercial interests wish us to buy and eat certain foods. Highly refined foods keep better than do natural foods; they are easier to store and ship. They cannot spoil because they cannot support the health of bacteria, fungi, molds, or weevils; certainly they cannot build human health either.

—Adelle Davis

ANNOUNCER: What's "The Profile"?

"The Profile" is looking like this so you get looked at like this.

When you have "The Profile" you not only make the scene, you steal it.

How can you keep "The Profile"?

By following the Profile Bread Menu Planner available at your grocer's.

The Profile Plan can help you keep slender.

And delicious Profile has no artificial sweeteners.

What have you got to lose—except tomorrow's weight.

—a television commercial

need substantially more exercise than we get. It will help your mental health and disposition, your posture, your intellectual powers, your sense of physical well-being, your sexual activity, your heart and circulatory system, your physical attractiveness, your capacity to sleep, and your weight control. It's possible to work exercise into your daily routine in ways that will take no additional time (or only marginally more). So what excuse have we got?

Food

Once you gain a sense of consciousness of your body, you are necessarily more careful of what you put into it. Few Americans have enough basic nutritional knowledge to be safe wandering about alone in supermarkets, restaurants, and drive-ins. Primitive man didn't have much nutritional knowledge either. But he didn't have to get his food from those sources. I am as partially informed and misinformed about nutrition as the next guy. At the time I was writing this book I was just beginning to read more about food and to buy more from whole-food stores.

So far, however, I think the rebuttable presumption is proving to be of greatest value to me in the area of food and nutrition. Primitive man didn't use artificial fertilizers and chemical insecticides, and, until someone can prove to my satisfaction that they make a positive contribution to my body, I'd prefer to avoid them. The same thing goes for chemical additives, especially those added to prevent spoilage ("to insure freshness"). Whole grains have more nutritional value than those man has treated, heated, "refined," and coated with sugar. (Have you ever noticed how they take the wheat germ *out* of your bread—along with most of its other

Analysis of a meteorite that fell in Kentucky has disclosed the ... 18 chemical "building blocks" of life ... known as amino acids, ... similar to those from which proteins are formed in life on earth.

—*The New York Times*

Our children are being programmed to demand sugar and sweetness in every food . . . are deliberately being sold the sponsor's less nutritious products and . . . are being counter-educated away from nutrition knowledge.

—Robert Choate

ANNOUNCER: The hurry-up, keep-up world of children. The hurry-up, keep-up world of children can make them tense and upset. This can cause irregularity despite proper diet. So when your child is irregular give him Fletcher's Castoria. This natural vegetable laxative is made specially for children in a hurry-up, keep-up world.

—a television commercial

natural goodness—and then sell it back to you?) Natural sweeteners like honey, or fruits, are better for you than that chemical white powder, called sugar, that the corporations are pushing. And fresh, raw fruits and vegetables are better for you than those that are cooked, canned, or frozen.

You can easily ignore most of the products in your supermarket and do a little more food preparation from basic ingredients yourself. Most of what I buy is fish, fresh fruits and vegetables. There is very little meat in my diet, except when it's served to company. There are powdered milk and fruit and vegetable juices. Honey is the sweetener. There are dried beans for soups, wheat germ, nuts, raisins, and oats for muesli, and whole-grain flour for bread. There are salt, baking soda, spices and herbs, vegetable oils, and vinegar. With this approach to food I can pass by not only individual products, but whole shelves and aisles. I do not buy: cold breakfast cereals, soft drinks, potato chips and comparable "munchies," candy and cookies, frozen or canned fruits and vegetables, or prepared dishes or meals (whether dry, canned, or frozen). It's a wonderfully liberating feeling to walk through an aisle of such junky, overpriced food of little nutritional value and realize that I don't *want* it.

I'm not interested in giving cooking or any of these other activities a lot of time, but cooking from scratch doesn't necessarily take longer. I can make corn bread with baking soda in about the same time it takes to go to the store, or put supper on the table (twenty-five minutes). But I won't take the time to make yeast bread, often, unless there's somebody there to visit with, or something else to do at the same time. I make

There's a whole new way of living. Pepsi helps supply the drive. It's got a lot to give to those who like to live 'cause Pepsi helps 'em come alive. It's the Pepsi Generation. Comin' at ya, goin' strong. Put yourself behind a Pepsi. If you're a livin', you belong. You've got a lot to live, and Pepsi's got a lot to give.

—a television commercial

Dr. Pauling suggested that many pharmaceutical manufacturers, medical journals and some physicians have tried over the years to quash the evidence that vitamin C is beneficial in preventing colds in order to maintain high profits. One-quarter of all advertisements in medical journals are related to the treatment of the common cold. Drug manufacturers earn $50-million a year selling remedies to the American public.

—The New York Times

my own muesli (rolled oats, wheat germ, raisins, etc.) in less time than it takes to open a box of Captain Crunch. But I don't often take the time to crack and pick walnuts to add to it.

The worst foods of all are those that are almost wholly the creation of man: cakes with refined sugar and flour and chemical additives to prevent molding; carbonated beverages with refined sugar and chemical sweeteners; potato slices or corn meal fried in saturated or hydrogenated (and possibly rancid) fats. Cream for your coffee? Not quite. Read the ingredients an airline stewardess gave me in a little plastic cup of chemical stuff called, beguilingly, "For Your Coffee." The cover reads in its entirety, in smaller print than the law permits in your insurance policy:

> Non dairy product. Ingredients: water, corn syrup solids, vegetable fat, sodium casenate, sodium citrate, polysorbate 68, sorbitan monostearate, mono- and diglycerides, carrageenan, artificial color, ETA, carotene. Distributed by United Air Lines, Inc., Chicago, Ill. 60666. Net ½ Fl. Oz. PULL

It is only a rebuttable presumption, mind you, but somebody is going to have to tell me why I should dump that little vial of chemicals into my body before *I'm* going to "PULL."

Needless to say, the same thing goes for the chemicals called "medicines." If a doctor orders me to consume a foreign substance, I'll either take it or get another doctor. But if a remedy can be found that does not involve drugs—exercise, improved nutrition, sleep, or massage—I'd sure opt for it.

In losing our capacity for play and in devaluing our imaginations, we have in a very important sense lost ourselves. The death of God in our world is the death of our capacity to experience the world in a godlike way: with the full release of our creative powers, valuing our experience of people and of things for their own sakes, with that sense of ease and timelessness we have when for the moment we are set free from anxiety and self-preoccupation.

—Marcia Cavell

Sit there. Don't smoke. Why must you smoke? Don't thumb a magazine. . . . You are missing the minute. And by missing the minute, you are missing everything, because all you have is that minute.

—Joan Baez

I get crazy and think I've
got to do things instead of just
letting them happen. Total
freedom is threatening. We all
say we want it, but when it
comes, it scares you.

—John Koehne

Time

Our lives and our jobs tend to encourage, or require, certain attitudes about time of which we are often unconscious. We have schedules and appointments; we "have to" do one thing or another by a particular time. This is very efficient in one sense. The output of the corporations is in many ways dependent on it. (And, if you are doing boring work you hate, it's about the only way to get through it; left to a more natural pace you'd simply never get out of the office.) But it's a very unnatural way to live.

If you take corporate stimulants like coffee, alcohol, and nicotine, stay up watching their television programs, and have to take one of their sleeping pills to get to sleep, you then have to use one of their alarm clocks to wake up. Once you begin to live more naturally, you go to bed when you get tired, wake up with the sunrise, and you don't need their alarm clocks.

If you are living a fully balanced life, you tend to get done all the things you need to do by doing them when you want to. You enjoy everything more, and you certainly accomplish as much—probably more. You are stimulated and enthusiastic (not bored); you are energetic (not listless). Yesterday when I was writing, I stopped to bake two loaves of whole-wheat bread. (I wrote up the new recipe in my journal.) I didn't have to (you can always put grain in your diet in other ways). I wanted a break and it was what I seemed to feel like doing at the time.

There are a lot of things I cannot accomplish without open-ended time. For example, I like to write in the mornings. If I've had a good night's sleep, I feel

The Japan that I foresee emerging will not be a country of rush and hurry, but a quieter place, where people will be contented to enjoy whatever fruits the best utilization of their capacity would produce.

—Nobutane Kiuchi

In fact artistic experience lies so incredibly close to that of sex, to its pain and its ecstasy, that the two manifestations are indeed but different forms of one and the same yearning and delight.

—Rainer Maria Rilke

For many years now, Western man—especially in the management world—has also worn clothing intended to discourage riotous conduct: the somber, sensible suit, white shirt, and dignified necktie, embodying businesslike propriety. But this . . . may soon lie shattered on the ground, and there is already hell to pay in the $20-billion U.S. men's wear business.

—Walter McQuade

good then. I don't clutter up my mind with newspapers, radio, television, or phonograph records. I just have my breakfast and get ready for the day, and pretty soon little thoughts come into my mind. Sometimes they just go in the journal, because they're of no particular use to anybody. Other times I'll type them out in the form of first-draft opinions, articles, speeches, testimony, or what not. But I can't just sit down and order myself to write. Nor can I do it knowing I'm going to have to stop at a fixed time. I may wake at 5:30 A.M. and have done all the writing I want to by 7:30. Or I may wake at 7:30 and write until noon. (Or, far more often than I would like, I have to leave for a commission meeting at a particular time.) Open-ended time is also essential for making love—or poetry (which are kind of the same thing).

Clothing

We've already discussed fashion somewhat. As I said, I don't particularly dig it. I wear the cheapest, most comfortable clothes I can find: old dress shirts (button down oxford cloth) from the office, old khakis, and hiking boots—or, if I'm about the apartment, some moccasins I made with my boys. If it's raining or chilly I wear a khaki jacket. If it's really cold, I have a sweat shirt with a hood, and gloves. I mean, that's what I like. I generally wear my "Commissioner uniform" (a business suit) at the office (though not always). Mason Williams once told me he changed his clothing style when his clothes were stolen after a concert in Detroit. He decided from then on he'd only buy and wear clothes nobody would want to steal.

I do some minor mending: buttons, ripped seams,

"The new freedom in dressing is fabulous," said Mrs. Norton Sloan, who had carefully keyed her multicolored sweatshirt to her denim shorts with a multicolored belt. "The only trouble is, you have to keep shopping to keep up with it."

"Like every week," agreed her friend, Mrs. Clive Summers, whose mauve boots matched her mauve shorts, jacket and huge canvas shoulder bag, all from Bergdorf Goodman's Biba shop.

—*The New York Times*

Of all the people I talked to, the most frustrated and angry were those trapped in spirit-numbing jobs and in neighborhoods besieged by pollution, noise, traffic, decay and crime. The happiest were those whose jobs gave them some relief from tedium, and a chance to live near open fields and green trees, sunlight, creeks and country roads.

—Karl Fleming

Commuter—one who spends his life
In riding to and from his wife;
A man who shaves and takes a train
And then rides back to shave again.

—E. B. White

and such. But I have never sewn any real clothes. I have a great admiration for people who can. Again, however, I think a woman (or man) who sews might want to try approaching it like cooking: experimenting a bit instead of copying precisely what some pattern and sewing-materials corporation is trying to get you to do exactly their way.

Shelter

What you live in and where you live are matters involving a tremendous range of personal choice—more than you might imagine you have. I met an architectural student at Windham College who fashioned a very elaborate tree house for himself off campus. My sister lived on a sailboat for a year. I wanted to live in an old, abandoned lock house on the C & O Canal, but the Park Service demurred. I am now living—as you may be—in a conventional American apartment house (three-story "garden type"). I like to live on the ground floor (so I can wheel my bicycle in and have easier access to the yard), and I sought out a place right across the street from one of Washington's wilderness parks (where I go for walks and cycle to work). I think it's important to have an accessible wilderness with which you are familiar through all the seasons.

Suburbs were invented by the automobile industry. The joy of living just far enough from your office to give you a regular walk or bicycle ride every day is hard to overestimate. It saves a tremendous amount of time and money. It helps to integrate your life for you psychologically. And it enables you to eliminate that classic corporate activity called commuting.

It's nice to have a room you can call your own,

In the background of all of this is the collective Self of the American people which has been educated to put the high-rising living standard in the place of true Self-realization.

—Jules Henry

To accumulate possessions is to deliver pieces of one-self to dead things. Possessions can absorb [emotions], but unlike personal relationships they feed nothing back.

—Philip Slater

well . . .
I cry when I see
that brand new
automatic washing machine
'cause
I'm sentimental
for the old machine
still yet
'cause the old one
really looked like a
real live washing machine
but the new one
just looks more like a
television set . . .

—John Hartford

whether you're living alone or with others. Beyond that, however—assuming you can afford more space—you may find that the less room you have the better. Our country's most fashionable suburbs house many people who either spend a disproportionate part of their time, energy, and money with their houses, or have contracted out so much of the work (gardening, cooking, etc.) that their homes take on a sterile hotel atmosphere.

I like to keep my home furnishings as simple, functional, and cheap as possible. As with fashion, I realize that mankind has for years wanted to make his dwelling aesthetically pleasing. Many women (and men) take great delight in interior decorating, and those who are original, artistic, and reasonably frugal about it have my admiration. But all too many simply buy the corporate standards for the interior decoration of their homes with the same lack of personal involvement they apply to the exterior decoration of their bodies. You can even buy an interior decorator.

I was going to make furniture out of some old trees brought back from West Virginia, but so far it hasn't happened. If you can't make your own furniture and other household objects, you can try to buy them from people who do. Fran Riecken, a woman I have known since I was a very small boy, has taken up pottery in the last few years—with non-toxic glazes. Her pieces are so nice that I really prefer the "seconds" because they look more handmade (and are cheaper). They are all about my office and home. I could easily get by with my four-place camp cook set and would never consider buying corporate dishware, but her batter bowls, plates, and cups add to my pleasure. Find the folks in your area who are into handicrafts: weaving, leatherwork,

It is assumed by the utilities that the demand for power is real because people continue to purchase it. However, we are all bombarded with massive amounts of advertising encouraging us to buy appliances, gadgets, new cars, and so on. There is no comparable public service advertising pointing up the harmful effects of over-purchase of "convenience" appliances that increase use of power.

—Garrett DeBell

If donning a sweater or adding a blanket to the bed at night is comfortable, lower the thermostat by a degree or two. Raising the setting only one degree costs 3% to 4% more in fuel consumption; raising it five degrees, 15% to 20% more.

—Paul Swatek

WHY EVERYONE SHOULD CONSERVE ELECTRICITY (AND OTHER THINGS, TOO)

Electricity is the cleanest form of energy used by man. But even electricity causes some damage to the environment—to air, water, and the landscape. We therefore urge that everyone conserve electricity at *all* seasons of the year. By "conserve" we mean: use what you need for healthful, safe, and pleasant living, but do not waste.

It may be more profitable for Con Edison if you burn unnecessary lights, over-heat and over-cool your apartment or home, and otherwise keep your meter running at full speed. But it costs you money. More seriously, it may cause unnecessary pollution, and waste precious natural resources.

—Consolidated Edison mailer

pottery, wood and metalworking. Give *them* your money. It will enrich your life, provide you some original and appreciated gifts for others, and help to create a community in which such activities can continue.

You might ask yourself with regard to any object, piece of clothing, or "thing": Can I do without it? Can I repair something I already have? Can I substitute something cheaper or simpler? Can I make it for myself? If not, can I buy it handmade from the craftsman? Only if all else fails do you shop for it, and then, when possible, at a small shop where you can deal personally with the owner.

Corporate box houses with bad ventilation (or no shade trees) and poor insulation (enormous glass doors and windows) need more heating and cooling than houses designed to fit their environment. Unless you're into wood stoves, you're going to have to buy the corporations' electricity (or gas, or oil, or whatever fuel they have decided to sell you). About all you can do to fight back is to use as little of it as possible. It will save you money, and be better for your health. In summer, use fans to push fresh air around. The excessive use of air conditioners has taken on social consequences. Occasionally heavy usage produces blackouts when the power companies overstrain their systems. Always it uses up the nation's limited energy resources. (Most of our electricity is being generated by processes that burn up coal, oil, and natural gas.)

Even lighting—once the exclusive preserve of sun and fire—has been taken over by the corporations. Artificial light has become a necessity in our homes and on the streets at night. But try turning off the lights during

Have a living Christmas tree.... There are two advantages of planting your holiday trees: you improve your landscaping, and you will have pleasant mementos.

—Betty Ann Ottinger

They took all the trees and put them in a tree
   museum
And they charged all the people a dollar and a half
   just to see 'em

—Joni Mitchell

In most cases the only really safe (or necessary) insecticides are birds and a fly swatter. . . . One purple martin can easily dispatch 2,000 mosquitoes in a single day.

—Betty Ann Ottinger

All I need to do is wake up
in the morning and hear the
birds. That gives me joy.

—Bill Scudder, an aircraft mechanic

the day whenever possible. Natural light is cheaper, prettier, and better for your eyes.

Plants are nice around the house, inside and out. They are life—in a world of plastic and cement. Gardening is the only modern-day tie for most of us to the life of our agrarian ancestors. Few of us can raise a significant proportion of the fruit and vegetables, let alone meat, we eat in a year. But you can generally find somewhere to plant a few carrots or radishes—even if it's in a window box or a flowerpot on the sill. I got permission to use a small plot of ground that was between a chain-link fence and the wall of my apartment house. Up the street, a number of apartment dwellers have substantial gardens on a plot provided by the Department of the Interior within the boundary of my park.

I also use my little garden plot to recycle some of my fruit and vegetable scraps. It's not clear what the owner or manager think, but in fact there is no unpleasant odor whatsoever (it's best not to include meat or fats) if the scraps are adequately buried and watered. It's really as important for me as for the soil—a sense of contribution to the earth that sustains us.

I like animals, too, but I would rather "keep" wild ones that can care for themselves in freedom than to buy one from a pet store and feed it corporate pet food. I hang birdhouses and feeders about and have never been at a loss for friendly animals.

Creativity and contemplation
From here on out, your life naturally evolves on its own. You were born to love, to be creative, to use your intellectual powers in freedom, to contemplate the wonder of things in a religious or philosophical way. That's

Each individual will find self-expression. All of life will become personal, artistic expression of one kind or another. The domestic arts will be the center of creation: building, gardening, cooking, decorating, entertaining; living well. Crafts will flourish such as weaving, sewing, pottery, woodwork, stonework, ironwork, etc.

—L. Clark Stevens

Almost every child, on the first day he sets foot in a school building, is smarter, more curious, less afraid of what he doesn't know, better at finding and figuring things out, more confident, resourceful, persistent and independent than he will ever be again in his schooling—or, unless he is very unusual and very lucky, for the rest of his life.

—John Holt

Education squashes my growth.

—Berger in *Hair*

Composing to a composer is like fulfilling a natural function. It is like eating or sleeping.

—Aaron Copland

not something you have to learn. It's something you have to get back to. You have to unlearn what the corporations have taught you. All you need is your freedom, the freedom to be yourself, to know yourself. You can't be free when you're a part of the corporate state: Your cells are composed of its chemicals; your body is covered with its sprays and clothes; you are transported along its freeways in its automobiles; you sit on its furniture, eat from its dishes, and fill your head full of its advertising and propaganda and manufactured entertainment.

Once you get all that stuff out of your system, what's left is you. Whistle an original tune. Better yet, try to work it out on your guitar. You will find yourself naturally writing thoughts and observations, fairly called "poetry," in your journal—not because you're suddenly a genius, but because you're suddenly human. You cannot possibly become intimate with a woods—to know its fog, to be there when the first morning sun arrives, to watch the lightning splatter its treetops as they whip about at night before a rain—without thinking some thoughts beyond yourself. To me it seems natural to wonder about the religious doctrines that have captured the imagination of man over the centuries. You will naturally come to reflect on your relationships with other people, too. You will try to be more honest in identifying and dealing with your feelings and those of others.

You, as a baby of a healthy and well-nourished mother, began life with good cellular structure, pink lungs, curiosity, and creativity. You would, naturally, learn to give and share love. Your curiosity would lead you to fill your mind with information. Your natural

This horn-of-plenty of benefits—from how to live without fighting to how to please your wife—all derive from
. . . understanding who you are, why you're here, how
you tick—and behaving accordingly. Happiness is functioning the way a being is organized to function. . . .

—Sam, in Robert A. Heinlein's
Stranger in a Strange Land

Let life happen to you. Believe me: life is right, in any
case. . . . Everything that makes *more* of you than you have
heretofore been in your best hours, is right. Every heighten-
ing is good if it is in your *whole* blood, if it is not intoxica-
tion, not turbidity, but joy which one can see clear to the
bottom.

—Rainer Maria Rilke

joy and enthusiasm would be expressed in creative ways. You could live off the earth. You would naturally seek out good food. Fresh air and clean water would help sustain you. You would not be wasteful of the land's abundance. You would be physically fit, naturally, from going about your daily rounds. You would be reflective about the meaning of your life and your relation to the earth. You *still* possess a little bit of all of these qualities. To the extent they are out of harmony with the life you lead, you feel the strain.

You had to be taught to demand heavy doses of refined sugar in your diet and other nonfood products and stimulants: soft drinks, coffee, and alcohol. You had to be sold the idea of filling your lungs with smoke. You had to have your curiosity and creativity pounded out of you by your parents and teachers. You have to be conned into buying the junk that clutters up your life—decreasing your happiness and your pocketbook. You have to be trained to be physically lazy.

You're all right. You can live on the earth just fine. You were made for it. You're welcome there. It's all that stuff that's been laid on you—at some corporation's profit—that's making you miserable and causing you to lose track of the rhythm of the earth. You can get it back. But only when you remember where you lost it.

We might have to slow down a little or perhaps even sit quiet occasionally to develop better taste. One can't think very deeply at 70 miles an hour.

—C. E. Warne

My new pattern requires renting new cars at the airports as needed. I am progressively ceasing to own things, not on a political-schism basis, as for instance Henry George's ideology, but simply on a practical basis. Possession is becoming progressively burdensome and wasteful and therefore obsolete.

——R. Buckminster Fuller

When you drive a car, you drive a reflection of yourself. And, in the case of the 1971 MGB, it's a reflection of someone very special.

—MG advertisement in *Time*

Antidote to Automobiles

So far, we have approached alternate life styles almost in terms of hedonism: What *feels* best for you? What will remove the pain of living in a corporate state —other than the drug life (whether alcohol, tranquilizers, or others) that only brings more ultimate pain? But what we so often discover is that the very products, activities, and attitudes that make you feel better also have significant social advantages: They use less of our nation's precious natural resources, they pollute less, they make less noise, they add to the pleasure of others, they enable each of us to live in a society in which we can grow in individual worth and fulfillment, they are more aesthetically pleasing, they make for better citizenship, and they are even more economical. Take bicycles, for example.

I ride a bicycle—not because I hate General Motors but haven't the courage to bomb an auto plant. I don't do it as a gesture of great stoicism and personal sacrifice. I am not even engaged, necessarily, in an act of political protest over that company's responsibility for most of the air pollution by tonnage in the United States. It's like finally giving up cigarettes. You just wake up one morning and realize you don't want to start the day with another automobile. Cigarette smoking is not a pleasure, it's a business. In the same way, you finally come to realize that you don't need General Motors, they need you. They need you to drive their cars for them. You are driving for Detroit and paying them to do it. Automobiles are just a part of your life that's over, that's all. No hard feelings. You've just moved on to something else. From now on you just use their buses, taxis, and rental cars when they suit your

The most natural form of locomotion, walking has been in use since before the invention of the wheel and the discovery of fire. Reliable and totally non-polluting, it offers convenience—no parking, no cost. Invigorating, it promotes health and gives you the chance to think.

—Paul Swatek

Automobiles insulate man not only from the environment but from human contact as well. They permit only most limited types of interaction, usually competitive, aggressive, and destructive. If people are to be brought together again, given a chance to get acquainted with each other and involved in nature, some fundamental solutions must be found to the problems posed by the automobile.

—Edward T. Hall

ANNOUNCER: Sidney spent Sundays she shelling at the seashore. Then Sidney started digging the Mustang—the great original. . . . Now Sidney's making waves all over. Last week he saved three bathing beauties. (And they all could swim better than Sidney!) Only Mustang makes it happen!

—a television commercial

convenience. You don't keep one for them that you have to house, feed and water, insure, and care for.

You ride a bicycle because it feels good. The air feels good on your body; even the rain feels good. The blood starts moving around your body, and pretty soon it gets to your head, and, glory be, your head feels good. You start noticing things. You look until you really see. You hear things, and smell smells, you never knew were there. You start whistling nice little original tunes to suit the moment. Words start getting caught in the web of poetry in your mind. And there's a nice feeling, too, in knowing you're doing a fundamental life thing for yourself: transportation. You got a little bit of your life back! And the thing you use is simple, functional, and relatively cheap. You want one that fits you and rides smoothly, but with proper care and a few parts it should last almost forever. Your satisfaction comes from within you, not from the envy or jealousy of others. (Although you are entitled to feel a little smug during rush hours, knowing you are also making better time than most of the people in cars.)

On those occasions when I am not able to cycle through the parks or along the canal—because the paths are rough with ice or muddy from rain or melting snow —bicycling enables me to keep closer to the street people: folks waiting for buses or to cross streets, street sweepers, policemen, school "patrols," men unloading trucks. Needless to say, you cannot claim any depth of understanding as a result of such momentary and chance encounters, but by the time I get to the office I do somehow have the sense that I have a much better feeling for the mood of the city that day than if I had come to my office in a chauffeur-driven government limou-

On a different speed scale, bicycles could move 2.8 times as many people per amount of space. If a bicycler can make 10 miles an hour, the car would have to exceed 28 mph to rack up more passenger miles on the same system of streets. But the New York City average speed for cars during rush hour is only 8.5 mph, 13 mph on the feeder roads. It's a fact that today in many cities you can make better time aboard a bicycle than in a car.

—Paul Swatek

Make your second car a bicycle.

Consider the advantages that the bicycle has to offer—low cost, no pollution, and convenient to park.

For under $50 you can get a bicycle fitted with enough trimmings to make it practical for going shopping and carrying a small child. The cheapest car costs about thirty times that.

A bicycle is also inexpensive to operate, maintain, and insure.

Bicycles are quieter than any form of motorized transportation, produce no pollution, and use up no fuel.

A bicycle takes up about 1/30th the parking space of a car.

In city traffic today, the bicycle is often faster than the car or bus.

Bicycles give the rider the sort of healthy exercise that many Americans usually do not get.

Riding a bicycle makes it possible to get a better appreciation of a beautiful day, or a pleasant ride through the park.

... *The New York Times* quoted a 32-year-old millionaire who pedals up Fifth Avenue to social engagements in a dinner jacket as explaining, "It's much easier than fussing with a chauffeur."

—Paul Swatek

sine. Although I am willing to brave the traffic and exhaust, I am aware it is dangerous. I think bicycles ought to be accorded a preferred position in the city's transportation system. At the very least, they deserve an even break.

Notice that bicycle riding also has some significant social advantages over the automobile. Cars unnecessarily kill sixty thousand people every year, permanently maim another one hundred and seventy thousand, and injure three and a half million more. The automobile accounts for at least 60 percent of the total air pollution in the United States by tonnage—as high as 85 percent in some urban areas—and 91 percent of all carbon-monoxide pollution; it creates about nine hundred pounds of pollution for every person every year. One million acres of land are paved each year; there is now a mile of road for each square mile of land. The concrete used in our Interstate Highway System would build six sidewalks to the moon. Even so, everyone is familiar with the clogged streets and parking problems —not to mention the unconscionable rates charged by the parking garages. Automobile transportation is the largest single consumer of the resources used in our nation's total annual output of energy. It is an economic drain on consumers—in no way aided by auto companies that deliberately build bumpers weaker than they were fifty years ago in order to contribute to an unnecessary bumper-repair bill in excess of one billion dollars annually.

The bicycle is a model citizen, by comparison.

The bicycle does not kill or maim; it does not pollute; it does not deplete natural resources; it makes no noise; it takes a great deal less space; and it is very much cheaper. (You can buy a brand new bicycle for

Commuting by bicycle? Is this some kind of put-on? It may sound like a joke to motor-minded America, but in the rest of the world nobody is laughing. In countries that are willing to take it seriously, the bicycle [is] transportation. Switzerland, for example, which traditionally places a high value on peace of mind and purity of air, has more bicycles than automobiles. In Amsterdam—a national capital with roughly the same population and climatic conditions as Washington, D.C.—150,000 people ride bikes to work every day. Hundreds of thousands more commute by bicycle in other European cities. The same is true in much of Africa and Asia.

—Thomas R. Reid, III

This year an estimated 10 million bicycles will be sold, compared to a projected 8.6 million new cars.

—Friends of the Earth

little more than what it costs to operate an automobile for two weeks.) Although the bicycle makes a direct assault on four great problems that plague the modern city—traffic, noise, parking, and pollution—urban planners have overlooked it in their search for solutions to the urban transportation crisis.

It is more than ironic that America can invest so much stock faith and rhetoric in the competitive marketplace of commerce and yet ignore the "marketplace of ideas" (to use a phrase by Mr. Justice Holmes) by tolerating the television monopoly that is used to merchandise Detroit's peculiar dreams of the appropriate automotive life style—with all that life style's attendant social ills. My own commission, the Federal Communications Commission, has been instrumental in encouraging broadcasters' censoring off the airwaves the messages from ecology groups (like Friends of the Earth) that would cry out against the urban devastation being wrought by Detroit's automobiles. (The FCC decision, fortunately, has been substantially reversed by the U.S. Court of Appeals.) In perhaps one of the greatest advertising overkills of all time, we Americans are being grossly oversold an automotive product and life style (bigger, faster, sexier cars) that we neither need nor may really want, and that will surely eventually kill us with its exhaust by-products and lethargy-induced heart attacks, if it does not get us first in a crash. This may serve the corporate profits of the automotive, oil, steel, cement, and road-building industries, but it is shortchanging the American people.

There are other ways to get around.

The unique powers and initiative of each individual must be rediscovered, and used as a basis for work which contributes to the good of the community, rather than melted down to the collectivist pot of conformity.

—Rollo May

A society built to man's measure will not just be one that serves him but one that gives him the opportunity to serve . . . the opportunity to do something for himself and others . . . the fulfillment that comes with the exercise of his talents.

—John Gardner

There is a new value system emerging in this country, starting with the youth but not limited to them. It is becoming one of the new facts of life for the rest of us to deal with. It challenges basic assumptions that we not only have taken for granted, but have virtually dominated our national life for most of our lives. When Calvin Coolidge in 1925 said, "The business of America is business," a thoughtful people nodded, "Why yes—that's right." Today's young people are saying, "That's not enough." Some are going further and saying, "Business is ruining America. Business is destroying our natural resources—polluting our air and our water—and why? To produce garbage—things we don't need—and must throw away to keep the economy going. It's a garbage economy, and we don't need it."

The people who talk that way are not all hippies and not all young. An increasing number of older people are raising questions like that; and a few of them have been doing it for a long time.

—Louis B. Lundborg

Working in a Corporate State

A few years ago I was honored to be asked to participate in a meeting at which the Reverend Jesse Jackson spoke at Howard University Law School in Washington. It was a time of considerable unrest throughout America, but especially in the black community. Reverend Jackson spoke for about an hour. He itemized the grievances of the nation's blacks, and he did it with feeling. And, needless to say, he endorsed some radical change and called upon the students to help. He said, "You can help with the revolution," but then he paused, and he added, "if you know law." He went on to emphasize the need for skills, for education, and, in this instance, for legal training.

By the mere fact of your having read this book so far, the odds are very good that you are a part of America's privileged class. (Scarcely more than 1 percent of the people of this country regularly purchase and read serious books.) Because of the information and education you have, you possess a disproportionate share of the power to shape this country. And, as the late President Kennedy used to say, "With great power goes great responsibility."

If you have cast your talents with America's largest two hundred corporations, it is going to take Ralph Nader—and thousands of other Americans who are working for what are really quite modest reforms—a whole lot longer to bring them about. If you drop out, someone else is going to have to carry your load. If you can join with us, it's going to be more effective—and more fun.

I hope you are going to be able to give your professional life to righting some of our nation's wrongs. Because they must be righted, and they can be righted.

By giving low priority to the amount of technical talent and money to be used for the care of human beings and their participation in productive work, American society has been sacrificing future generations.

—Seymour Melman

By the time [a worker is] fifty, he's all worn out. Someone hands him some small pension and if he ain't half dead already from heart trouble or if he ain't a drunk, he's got about five years of watching TV to look forward to. That's life, friend.

—a welder

You get to the point where you stare at the rivets and to make the job mean something you start counting them like counting sheep. When you do that, you better watch out. Some guys tell you that means you're going crazy. So when it happens to me, I just go and watch television until I can come back and face it again. My kid looks at me and says, "Dad, what're you doing home again?" I tell him, "Listen, kid, you're going to college one day. You just won't understand it." I can never explain it to him.

—Willie Sanders, a thirty-seven-year-old riveter

We are making some progress. In fact, victory is inevitable. The very fact that we have to fight today for what the Declaration of Independence demanded two hundred years ago is itself a radicalizing phenomenon. We either win an individual skirmish, or the fact that we lose to the forces of greed and repression is so outrageous that more and more people are turned on to the need for change. The blind insensitivity of many of our nation's institutional leaders, their preposterous reactions to the mildest of sensible suggestions, is the best guarantee of change.

You may seek out a public interest organization to work for, or you may start your own. But maybe you either can't, or won't. Nevertheless, you may not be prepared to sell out deliberately either, to rip off what you can, and live out the Madison Avenue-Hollywood dream.

Thus far, this book has been limited to a consideration of "life." But most of us spend over half our waking hours at "work," our jobs. How do you stay free as a member of a large, bureaucratized institution? How do you avoid the depersonalization of patterned jobs, of work you don't care about, of a life style leading nowhere except to an early death of mind and spirit, if not body?

Newsweek devoted a special report to what it called the "Blue-Collar Blues"—the alienation of blue-collar workers. I think we are going to see more of that alienation and not just among so-called blue-collar workers. I don't think college by itself is the answer. There are a lot of college graduates who are doing the equivalent of staring at rivets. No, we have to learn to fight back, to find some tactics for survival in the corporate state.

Mrs. Graske: I'd say most of the girls get an upset stomach. I know I did as a telephone operator. So I take Rolaids. It's a very nerve-wracking job. And when things get hectic—acid goes up. There's heartburn. And pretty soon gas causes such pressure. It makes you feel bad. So I take Rolaids. For me it's an instant worker. They give my stomach a cool feeling. I don't know what Rolaids has, whatever it is—it works.

—a television commercial

The aim of ever-increasing consumption creates, even before the optimal consumption level is reached, an attitude of greed in which one wishes not only to have one's legitimate needs fulfilled but dreams of a never-ending increase in desires and satisfactions. In other words, the idea of the limitless rise of the production and consumption curve greatly contributes to the development of passivity and greed in the individual, even before peak consumption is reached.

—Erich Fromm

One tactic is simply to ignore your job. For many people, work is an empty, more or less painless means to the end of material resources. Life is built out of the time that is left—whether it is activities with the family, or a hobby, or even a second job, like farming, that may be more satisfying. The ethic of work for its own sake is rejected by such people. Work is like a dentist's appointment: something no one looks forward to, but that you can tolerate and is worth the trouble because it is a necessary preliminary to doing the other things you want to do. This is not a particularly appealing tactic, but without some fundamental changes it may be all that many people can look forward to. And it is surely to be preferred to the process of self-deception in which a worthless value structure and the approval of others commandeers your life through a job that is not worth doing.

Another tactic requires the resolve that you are not going to be a willing pawn for the life style that fuels the factories and, at the same time, fills the streams and air and earth with the discards of last year's products that no one needed or really wanted. Once you really *feel* the reasons why you don't want all that material fluff junking up your life, you find that you can get along on a lot less income, which in turn opens up many more alternatives for employment. You don't have to join a traditional institutional organization when you take a job. For example, the large law firms that represent mostly large corporations are finding it increasingly difficult to attract and hold the best that law schools have to offer, despite rising salaries and the worsening job situation in a recession economy. Graduates prefer a job at half or one-third the pay to

If there is one thing that is clear as we enter the 1970's, it is that the new generation of educated men and women will make sweeping demands of the institutions they come in contact with. The fashion and entertainment industries were revolutionized by their tastes; the colleges, the graduate schools, law firms and businesses have learned in turn that they must adjust to the values and beliefs of this new generation.

—David Broder

The easiest thing would have been to stay, [but] I couldn't create anything. The trade of one minute is forgotten the next. I didn't want to spend the rest of my life being unable to see anything I had done.

—a former New York stockbroker

Doing the same thing every day for decades is deadening. . . . Fifty acres of land can't stand up to the harassment of being planted in nothing but wheat, and people can't take that kind of harassment either.

—a former insurance man

do something worthwhile, rather than a job that pays a lot but does little or nothing for the country or themselves. The same is true in every discipline, as employees begin to ask not "How much do you pay?" but "What do you do, and why?"

Another tactic for those who find themselves inside a corporate or institutional setting, where change is reasonably possible, is to work for that change. It may be a small thing: how you wear your hair. It may be a bigger thing: day-care centers for children or a new minorities hiring policy. It may strike at the corporate heart: altering advertising claims or even a product line, reducing pollution, or adding safety devices. You can at least try to humanize the place: let employees have more choice about when they work; increase training opportunities and job rotation; give employees more responsibility for whole projects; encourage dissent, art on the walls, pets in the halls, athletic facilities, bicycle racks, and showers.

"Okay," you say, "neat idea; but how do I go about it?" The tactics probably aren't much different from what you may have already experienced in student or political action. You may well know a lot more about it than I do. And, in any event, your technique will have to vary from one institution and time to another. But these would seem to be useful fundamentals.

First of all, you have to have a sense of self, of your own individuality and worth, of what it is you are trying to accomplish and why. That is essential. If you are not sure who you are, if you think you would like to combine a life of maximizing material possessions with a little do-goodism from time to time, you are going to be too malleable. Arguments that you are "jeopardizing

Organizations oppress you.... They hold you down. I felt as if industry were consuming me. It took what it wanted but didn't put anything back. It doesn't allow you to grow as a person. You can grow in its image, but that's the only way. I don't admire the guy who's president of a company anymore. In fact, I feel pretty sorry for him.

—a former corporate engineer

Job vulnerability is obviously a critical psychological factor in the mind of a potential whistle-blower, and it will probably become more so as large organizations come to dominate an increasing portion of the nation's employment. The modern jilted employee cannot return to Monticello or become a self-made husbandman with ease. If he becomes a damaged good, tainted by a reputation as an organizational squealer, he may find so many doors locked that a drop in station or a change in profession will be required for grocery money.

—Taylor Branch

your future here," or that you should "go a little easier," or that "we are working these things out gradually," will sway you.

Second, you have to get a sense of the lay of the land. Who has the power in the organization? How is it exercised? Where are the pressure points? Is there a grievance machinery, a union or other organization of employees? Read everything you can get your hands on: employee manuals, annual reports, bulletin boards, newsletters, and press releases. Walk the halls to find out how the place is laid out physically, and what facilities, functions, and people it contains.

Third, you have to put together a program of demands. What, precisely, do you want? This is not an easy task.

Fourth, if there's not an employee organization, start one. Institutions prefer to deal with other institutions rather than human beings. Seek out people of like mind—at the water cooler, in the snack bar, at the next desk, after hours. Get it together—even if there are only a few of you.

Fifth, it's generally useful to process your suggestions or demands through channels. This is not because the established bureaucratic machinery will work—it's generally operated to encourage harassment, delay, and tokenism—but because it is very useful to be able to show that it doesn't work.

Sixth, it's then a good idea to lay your grievances on whomever is at the top. Sometimes these guys respond to common sense because they are more broadly educated and experienced; at other times they are cowardly, frightened of losing their jobs, and can't say no. In either event, you may get results.

People are encouraged to stay in the same job by pension plans and seniority systems, and actively discouraged from leaving by the knowledge that with age their desirability elsewhere diminishes. Yet it seems self-evident that after working incessantly for 10 years at the same job a person's enthusiasm for work becomes stale, his imagination stagnant, and that the only way to counteract this process of diminishing returns would be to take a long breather involving education or rest and possibly a decision to change fields or at least direction.

—Suzannah Lessard

Tell me, my patient friends, awaiters of messages,
From what other shore; from what stranger,
Whence, was the word to come?
Who was to lesson you?

. . .

Open your eyes! There is only earth and the man!

There is only you. . . .

—Archibald MacLeish

It is possible to remain human in an inhuman society . . . though one may have the best reasons in the world to destroy that world . . . one may choose not only not to destroy it, but to go on working, speaking and rebelling on its behalf.

—Elie Wiesel

Seventh, from here on out, if all else has failed, I'll leave it to your imagination. "Different strokes for different folks." There are countless examples of individual action and individual responsibility. Taylor Branch has written an article in the *Washington Monthly* in which he catalogues actions of conscience by "whistle blowers"—men and women who expose the crimes and failings of their own institutions. The exposé may take the form of a resignation, with an explanatory press conference, a letter to Ralph Nader or Jack Anderson, or may even be the basis for a full-dress congressional investigation. The article describes numerous examples, including the C5-A airplane excess costs and the cyclamate peril.

I do not offer my advice lightly, or with the assumption that things will go easily. Whistle blowing can be a very expensive occupation. You will need to expect and accept that life, especially your work life, will be unpredictable.

Above all, this is a time when individuals are needed. We have seen what individuals, acting in full understanding of their abilities and the claims of their conscience, can do. There was Martin Luther King and the countless individuals he inspired to fight racism in their daily lives. There was Robert Kennedy and the students who believed that the interests of the blacks, and the poor, and farmers, and workingmen could override deep-seated and irrational antagonisms to a better America. There is Ralph Nader, who has worked from within the system to show us how, one at a time, each of us can help to tame the corporate tiger that is ravishing our land and people.

In the end, we are each individually responsible for

The extraordinary thing about this new consciousness is
that it has emerged out of the wasteland of the Corporate
State, like flowers pushing up through the concrete pave-
ment. . . . For one who thought the world was irretriev-
ably encased in metal and plastic and sterile stone, it
seems a veritable greening of America.

—Charles A. Reich

If there's something called a revolution in the U.S. it
will not be a quick palace revolution but a long-term one, a
deep-going one, not in a city like Washington but all over
the country at once—in revolutionizing the way people live
day to day and the way they relate to one another.

—Howard Zinn

what we do, what happens in our lives and the lives of the people we touch, and the events in which we participate. There is no "silent majority." As the bumper sticker says, "The majority isn't silent, the government is deaf." There is no "mass" television audience. There are no bloc votes. There are only individuals who have considered and decided where they wish to be counted on the great issues of the day, and how they wish to live their lives.

When many individuals alter their lives, it begins to have social, economic and political consequences. Annual sales of bicycles appear now to be surpassing those for automobiles. Whether the bicycle becomes a meaningful form of urban transportation is affected to some degree by whether you ride one to work—and demand bicycle streets and parking facilities. The population explosion is a matter of how many children you decide to have. The social responsibility of the institutions you work for will be affected by the protests you lodge. The products manufactured by American corporations will be affected by your personal buying habits. (Levi's sales are still doubling every five years.) And—by no means of least importance—the future political course of this country will be affected by your willingness to register and vote, to work for, and contribute money to, the candidates of your choice.

Once the religious, the haunted and weary
Chasing the promise of freedom and hope
Came to this country to build a new vision
Far from the reaches of kingdom and Pope
The spirit it was freedom and justice
Its keepers seemed generous and kind
Its leaders were supposed to serve
    the country
But now they don't pay it no mind

  —Jerry Edmonton, John Day, and Nick St. Nicholas

Yes a new world's coming
The one we've had visions of
And it's growing stronger with each
    day that passes by
Coming in peace, coming in joy, coming
    in love.

      —Barry Mann and Cynthia Weil

Voting in a Corporate State

The times *are* changing. A new world *is* coming. And the surface indicia—hair styles, dress, music, sexual attitudes—are in many ways the least significant aspect of all. Everywhere people are trying to alter and humanize life for themselves, their families, and friends.

- A number of artists have created types of art which by their very nature could not be shown in galleries, such as the "earthworks" movement, conceptual art with no conventional display forms, or outsized canvases and monumental sculptures. Other artists have sought alternatives to the gallery system by simply finding other places to exhibit.

- In an attempt to alter family structure and experiment with community responsibility for child rearing, about ten collectively owned and supervised nurseries have been organized in New York City in the past year, and others are springing up around the country.

- Source Coalition is a Washington, D.C. collective of ten people living and working together on one salary and food stamps. They are developing a series of catalogues which will serve as a guide for the alternative movement and community organizers —groups, projects, magazines, films, books, and tapes. Earth Liberation Front toured the country by bus providing and gathering information on Alternative America. When they acquired more information than they could carry, they decided to publish the catalogues.

- One out of every three United States citizens owns shares in or works for one or more cooperatives; co-ops sold $477 million worth of goods and services in 1969.

The Revolution will not be televised.
The Revolution will not be right back
    after a message about the white tornado,
    white lightning, or white people.
You will not have to worry about a dove
    in your bedroom, the tiger in your tank,
    or the giant in your toilet bowl.
The Revolution will not go better with Coke.
The Revolution will not fight germs
    that might cause bad breath.
The Revolution *will* put you in the driver's seat.

The Revolution will not be televised,
    will not be televised, *not* be televised.
The Revolution will be no re-run, brothers.
The Revolution will be live.

—Gil Scott-Heron

The search of the youth today is for ways and means
to make the machine—and the vast bureaucracy of the
corporation state and of government that runs that machine—the servant of man.

That is the revolution that is coming.

—William O. Douglas

All over the world like a fever, freedom is spreading in
the widest liberation movement in history. The great masses
of people are determined to end the exploitation of their
races and lands. They are awake and moving toward their
goal like a tidal wave.

—Martin Luther King, Jr.

- In 1970, home sewing accounted for almost $2.5 billion in sales.

- Since 1964, the number of men over twenty-one who smoke declined from 53 to 42 million; those who have quit has gone from 22 to 33 million.

- In 1969, 412,690 mobile homes, new and used, were sold, accounting for a reported 46 percent of the single-family dwelling sales for that year.

These examples say, more effectively than I can, that (1) there are an awful lot of Americans of diverse backgrounds who are concerned about the impact of corporate pursuits on the quality of life; (2) we all have a lot more in common than our leaders and the mass media permit us to see; and (3) a great many of us are working out individual lives for ourselves that are, in fact, harmonious variations on the same themes.

Nevertheless, I disagree with Charles Reich in his prediction that individuals' greening is going to bring the downfall of the corporate state. I think not. Meaningful reforms are still going to require more conventional political action and legislation. There are going to continue to be an awful lot of people who, for a variety of reasons, can't or won't break out of the corporate trap. They would rather continue to tell themselves that they really want to drive that car, and smoke those cigarettes, and use that hairspray. Under it all may be the fear that if they went out in search of themselves they might come back empty handed. Almost any alternative is preferable to that nightmare.

It's not just that we don't like what our government's doing and want to change it. That's to be expected in a democracy. The dangerous thing is the extent to which people are turned off to government

I can't help feeling this would be a better country if we all leveled with each other. I don't hold a man's views against him so long as he tells me what they are. All politicians learn to sugarcoat the truth. I don't believe 90 percent of what they say. I guess they look down on the ordinary American workingman. I guess they don't trust us. I guess they figure they can con us, all the time con us.

—a gas station attendant

What this country needs is a "New Populism." We need "a positive coalition" to bring the hardhats and the students, and Americans everywhere, black, white, red, and yellow, together again.

—Fred Harris

I believe this country is made for the rich. The tax laws are written for them, and they hire those high-priced lawyers who can get you out of anything. It's the little guy who suffers; it's the little guy who works like a dog and keeps the country going. I'll tell you, I feel sorry for the colored person. They've had an awful time in this country. Sometimes I wonder how I'd feel if I was colored. Sometimes I stop and think: They do the dirty work in this country—just like I do.

—a policeman

We must remember that we are bound together as a people not by brute force, or ethnic homogeneity or geographic compactness. We are bound together by a common faith that ours is a nation which is trying to assure to all its citizens the rights of life, liberty and the pursuit of happiness. If that faith is shattered, we will have lost what no weapons and no armies can ever secure us.

—Edward M. Kennedy

altogether. The troublesome polls are not those that tell us half the American people think Nixon is doing a bad job as president. Nixon has brought us together—in spite of Agnew. Hardhats, students, and farmers stood shoulder-to-shoulder in Des Moines protesting the president's policies. No, the alarming polls are those that report the growing number of Americans who believe themselves totally alienated from the mainstream of American society.

Even those who support the two major parties have little enthusiasm for them, as the 1970 elections demonstrated. There is, today, none of the spirit that a Roosevelt, a Kennedy, or even a roughhewn president like Truman, could bring forth from the people.

The enthusiasm is for individuals; almost any individuals. There has been a common thread through much of the support for men as seemingly disparate as Barry Goldwater, George Wallace, Eugene McCarthy, Robert F. Kennedy, and George McGovern. They are all individuals, courageous and outspoken.

People know what's wrong. Listen to the taxi drivers, the waitresses, the filling-station attendants, the factory workers. They can speak with considerable eloquence about corporate and other institutional pressures. They see through a politician whose solution to inflation is to slash away at appropriations for education the same week he urges billion-dollar weapon systems. They've tried to fish in the polluted streams. They've had to return the defective and overpriced goods.

We have long passed the time when concern for the real quality of human life can be dismissed as mere romanticism, or naive idealism. Not only do we have

They're only puttin' in a nickel
And they want a dollar song
Oh yeah they're only puttin' in a little to get
    rid of a lot that's wrong.

Well I don't know so many things
But I know what's been goin' on
We're only puttin' in a little to get rid of a lot
    that's wrong.

                —Melanie Safka

It is my very strong feeling that real pacifism, real positive political change, cannot be effectively motivated by guilt, but must come instead from a joyful reverence for life, from a fervent desire to make our own lives more glorious and more ecstatic, and from the very *selfish* desire to share that joy with all the people and all the living things of the universe.

                —Mayer Vishner

Give people bread and
let them make their own
circuses.

        —Paul Goodman

The world needs a reason to clap its
    hands.
The world needs a leader for its band.

        —Red Lane, Larry Henley, and Johnny Slate

the economic opportunity to create a self-fulfilling society, not only do we have the moral imperative to do so, but we are confronted with the political and social necessity of doing so if we are not to perish in our own self-inflicted violence and insanity.

I don't mean to detract from the issues of the 1960's, which are still very much with us. We simply must stop the bloodbath in Southeast Asia. We must substantially increase spending for the obvious domestic needs—poverty, employment, education, housing, environmental control, medical services, and hunger. We must recognize the rights of *all* our minority groups —104 million women; 20 million over sixty-five years of age; 20 million under five; blue-collar workers—not just Blacks, Chicanos, and Indians. None of this can be accomplished without making corporations more responsive to all of us, consumers, employees, and shareholders. All of it would be aided by meaningful decentralization: "participatory democracy."

But, for the 1970's, I think we are looking for more, much more. First, we want to find ourselves; to become more fully human. That single goal pervades a great deal of the highly disparate kind of searching we are witnessing today. We seek a moral purpose to life, a vision, idealism, truth, love, excitement. Second, we want a return to old values—not necessarily of our parents, but of our grandparents. All about us—in furniture, clothes, entertainment, the return to nature—we see the nostalgic looking back to a simpler life. We are coming to reject the very corporate life style being sold by the major corporate contributors to both parties. And I think any party, or candidate, who fails to recognize these facts will have little political influence.

What [young people] ... say they want doesn't sound so different, you know, from what our Founding Fathers said they wanted—the men who wrote our Declaration of Independence, our Mayflower Compact, the Bill of Rights, the other early documents that laid the foundation of the American Dream. They said they wanted the freedom to be their own man, the freedom for self-realization. We have lost sight of that a bit in this century—but the young people are prodding us and saying, "Look, Dad—this is what it's all about."

—Louis B. Lundborg

Perhaps most disheartening of all, is the way consumers are demonstrating their disaffection with the average commercial break—by simply walking away from the set. In early days, between 1961 and 1963, it was normal to lose an average of 15–18 percent of our audience automatically when the commercials came on. Our latest information indicates that last year, when commercials interrupted the program an average of 27 percent of the people had left their sets before we even got on the air. Sometimes departures ran as high as 50 percent.

—Edward H. Meyer

The American people may not be calling for revolution in the classic sense, but they are calling for some straight talk. We don't want the government overthrown, we just want it to stop tapping our telephone. We don't want to declare war on our government, we just want it to stop waging undeclared wars on other governments. We don't mind paying taxes, we just don't like taxing the poor to fatten the rich.

We want something useful to do. We don't want to have to use up our civic pride and energy preventing our government's ill-considered actions—keeping the Supreme Court free of Carswells and the sky free of SSTs.

We are willing to work for good government, but we shouldn't have to outbid ITT in our effort to *buy* publicly responsive officeholders.

How can the two major parties—as presently funded—offer solutions? They are the problem. There is *no way* to raise millions of dollars from big corporations for a campaign and elect officials who will represent the people who are manipulated, oppressed, and employed by those corporations. There is *no way* to fashion honest speeches and legislation about pollution that strikes a compromise with polluters who are a major source of campaign funds. There is *no way* to "clear" with the industry appointments to regulatory commissions that will then regulate them. There is *no way* to debate the issues freely with the electorate while corporate television controls the time available to candidates and officials.

But the total corporate domination of television—television entertainment, politics, and commercial messages—is producing a backlash. Every child knows that television lies to him. (One survey found that 20

Nine years ago, Newton Minow was shrugged off when he warned TV was selling our kids short. . . . Now . . . critics ask—"How much of their contempt for American institutions is a backlash against the crassness projected at them from the TV tube?"

—Stanley Cohen

All men . . . are endowed . . . with
certain unalienable Rights . . . Life,
Liberty, and the pursuit of Happiness.
To secure these rights, Governments are
instituted among Men. . . .
    Our repeated Petitions have been answered
only by repeated injury. A Prince, whose
character is thus marked by every act which
may define a Tyrant, is unfit to be the
ruler of a free people. . . . Whenever any
Form of Government becomes destructive . . .
it is the Right of the People to alter or
to abolish it. . . .

—*Declaration of Independence*

percent of the people who watched Nixon talk to the astronauts during their televised walk on the moon believe the astronauts were never there.) In the course of selling products to America, as Mason Williams has observed, "Big Business has created an America that will no longer buy its products. Their how blew their what." Because politicians in the age of multimillion-dollar campaigns are just another product "brought to you by" the largest corporations, people don't believe the politicians either. In short, whether 1972 is the year or not, the time is coming when the American people will no longer buy packaged politicians.

Somebody's going to start telling it straight in this country. Somebody's going to bare his soul and offer a human being to the American people. Somebody's going to do it at the corporations' expense—not on their expense accounts. Somebody's going to recognize that politics alone is not enough, that the people want a whole life—a party of life.

And when that happens, he—or she—is going to win.

Conclusion

My generation constitutes the straggling last remains of the puritan ethic, inner-directed old Americans. I can recall as a child the arrival of "civilization" at my uncle's Iowa farm: electricity for the lights and water pump instead of kerosene lanterns and the windmill; a fancy stove to replace the old cast-iron potbelly we fed corncobs and coal; indoor plumbing and a hot-water heater to replace the outhouse and the heating of bath water on the stove. Those were days of family ties, hard work, some hard times, Franklin Roosevelt, "The War," the Fourth of July, and genuine American patriotism taught you by grateful immigrant grandparents. I was young, but I was alive and aware, and I have some feeling for the confusion, frustration, and fears that many of my older family and friends express today.

No age is easy; but being in one's thirties at this time is especially difficult. You are caught between cultures. The temptation is to take sides, to move either forward or backward in time. The challenge is to stand firm, to try to discover as precisely as you can your honest-as-possible-self, to pick the best from all possible worlds, and to try to encourage constructive communication between two generations that seem to be missing most of what the other is saying. That is what many my age realize to be their responsibility and their opportunity; it is what I am trying to do.

What all of us need to learn, more effectively than any of us have so far, is what we have in common as a people. Four examples: When children reject the standards and life styles of their parents, what they are sometimes substituting instead turns out to be pretty close to the value system of their grandparents. Whether or not "God is dead"—in the sense that organized, institutionalized religion is failing to respond to the needs of people in this age—it is clear that religion is not dead (in the sense of a personal quest for a meaning in life beyond the daily routine). Those who are turning away from corporate jobs are often opting for harder and more meaningful work, not lethargy. Young people are not the only Americans who enjoy music, physical activity, poetry, and the great outdoors.

Nobody has "the" answer. Certainly I don't. Moreover, the answer changes—for each of us, over time, in different places. America's answer will only be found when two-hundred million individuals find two-hundred million individual answers.

Perhaps it is safe to suggest, however, that the best answers involve a sense of unity, of wholeness, of centering, of interconnectedness—"the whole thing." Buying, and putting in place, the pieces in corporate America's jigsaw puzzle of conspicuous consumption doesn't seem to have that quality of purpose or unity. There *is* an alternative, which many believe to be more "natural," that seems to work better for me. It centers on the life force that binds all of us to each other, and the universe from which we came and to which we return. It encourages individual growth and attainment of potential. It encourages simplicity in relation to things, and a richness in relation to people. It seeks to integrate creativity and contemplation, love, religion, exercise, food, clothing, shelter, transportation (life-support activities), relation to nature, and professional productivity into a balanced life in the city that comes as close as possible to the kind of integrated whole life man lived when first on earth.

But there is no formula. The purpose of self-discovery is not to stop copying Howard Johnson and to start copying Nick Johnson—or anybody else. The point is to find your own soul and kick it, poke it with a stick, see if it's still alive, and then watch which way it moves. Do it your way. Because you must. And because it's best. But don't forget to write and tell me how it all worked out.

Bibliography

This is a selected list of books that have some relation to this one: they deal with similar theories, they influenced me at some point in my life, they were written by friends who have influenced me, they are useful "workbooks" of some sort, guides to our culture, or they were blowing in the intellectual and emotional wind at the time this book was being put together. Many have been omitted. The list includes virtually none of the books I use professionally, and I deliberately listed only paperbacks.

JOAN BAEZ, *Daybreak* (Avon, 1969 [1966], 95¢).

RICHARD J. BARNET, *The Economy of Death* (Atheneum, 1969, $2.95).

The Bhagavad Gita (Penguin, 1962, 95¢).

ROLLIN AND MARCHA BINZER, *Understanding Why You Are Disappointed A Little Alone A Little Afraid and Nothing Seems Right Anymore* (The Communication Gap, 1971).

ERNEST CALLENBACH, *Living Poor with Style* (Bantam, 1972, $1.95).

CARLOS CASTANEDA, *The Teachings of Don Juan: a Yaqui Way of Knowledge* (Ballantine, 1968, 95¢).

PADDY CHAYEFSKY, *The Latent Heterosexual* (Bantam, 1967, 95¢).

HARRY H. CLARK (ed.), *Thomas Paine: Selections* (Hill and Wang, rev. ed., 1961, $2.45).

ELDRIDGE CLEAVER, *Soul on Ice* (Dell, 1968, 95¢).

ROBERT COLES AND JON ERIKSON, *The Middle Americans* (Atlantic-Little, Brown, 1971, $3.95).

The Constitution of the United States of America (Government Printing Office, 1968 [1789], 10¢).

Consumer Reports (P. O. Box 1000, Mt. Vernon, N.Y.; $8.00 a year, $6.00 for five or more subscriptions together).

EDWARD F. COX, ROBERT C. FELLMETH, JOHN E. SCHULZ, *The Nader Report on the Federal Trade Commission* (Grove Press, 1969, $1.25).

Tom Cuthbertson, *Anybody's Bike Book* (Ten Speed Press, 1971, $3.00).

Adelle Davis, *Let's Eat Right to Keep Fit* (Signet, 1954, $1.50).

Erich Fromm, *The Art of Loving* (Bantam, 1956, 75¢).

John Kenneth Galbraith, *The Affluent Society* (Mentor, 1958, 75¢).

John W. Gardner, *Self-Renewal* (Harper, 1965 [1963], $1.45).

Dwight Goddard (ed.), *A Buddhist Bible* (Beacon, 1970 [1938], $3.95).

Paul Goodman, *Growing Up Absurd* (Vintage, 1956, $1.95).

Søren Hansen and Jesper Jensen with Wallace Roberts, *The Little Red Schoolbook* (Pocket Books, 1971 [1969], $1.25).

John Hartford, *Word Movies* (Doubleday, 1971, $2.95).

Robert A. Heinlein, *Stranger in a Strange Land* (Berkley, 1961, $1.25).

Hermann Hesse, *Steppenwolf* (Bantam, 1969, $1.25).

Wendell Johnson, *Verbal Man* (Collier, 1965 [1956], 95¢).

Jacqueline Killeen (ed.), *Ecology at Home* (101 Productions, 1971, $1.95).

Yeffe Kimball and Jean Anderson, *The Art of American Indian Cooking* (Avon, 1965, 95¢).

Alicia Bay Laurel, *Living on the Earth* (Vintage, 1970, $3.95).

Alan Levy, William B. Chapman, Richard Saul Wurman, *Our Man-Made Environment Book Seven* (MIT Press, 1970, $4.95).

Marshall McLuhan, *Understanding Media* (McGraw-Hill, 1964, $1.95).

Rollo May, *Man's Search for Himself* (Signet, 1953, $1.25).

Donella H. Meadows, Dennis L. Meadows, Jorgen Randers, William W. Behrens, *The Limits to*

Growth: A Report for the Club of Rome (Potomac Associates-Universe, 1972, $2.75).

MORTON MINTZ AND JERRY S. COHEN, *America, Inc.* (Dell, 1972 [1971], $1.50).

ROBIN MORGAN (ed.), *Sisterhood Is Powerful* (Vintage, 1970, $2.45).

HELEN AND SCOTT NEARING, *Living the Good Life* (Schocken, 1954, 1970, $2.25).

The New English Bible (Cambridge, 1971, $4.45).

THE O. M. COLLECTIVE, *The Organizer's Manual* (Bantam, 1971, $1.25).

GEORGE ORWELL, *1984* (Signet, 1949, 95¢).

BETTY ANN OTTINGER, *What Every Woman Should Know—and Do—About Pollution* (Ep Press, 1970).

VANCE PACKARD, *The Waste Makers* (Pocket Books, 1960, 95¢).

LINUS PAULING, *Vitamin C and the Common Cold* (Bantam, 1971 [1970], $1.25).

ELIOT PORTER, *In Wildness Is the Preservation of the World* (Sierra Club-Ballantine, 1962, $3.95).

GEROME RAGNI AND JAMES RADO, *HAIR* (Pocket Books, 1966, 95¢).

CHARLES A. REICH, *The Greening of America* (Bantam, 1970, $1.95).

KENNETH REXROTH, *One Hundred Poems from the Japanese* (New Directions, 1964, $1.75).

RAINER MARIA RILKE, *Letters to a Young Poet* (Norton, rev. ed. 1954 [1934], $1.25).

ROBERT H. RIMMER, *The Harrad Experiment* (Bantam, 1966, $1.25).

ROBERT RODALE (ed.), *The Basic Book of Organic Gardening* (Organic Gardening-Ballantine, 1971, $1.25).

THEODORE ROSZAK, *The Making of a Counter Culture* (Anchor, 1968, $1.95).

JERRY RUBIN, *Do It!* (Simon & Schuster, 1970, $1.25).

SWAMI SATCHIDANANDA, *Integral Yoga Hatha* (Holt, 1970, $4.95).

MICHAEL SHAMBERG, *Guerilla Television* (Holt, 1971, $3.95).

PHILIP SLATER, *The Pursuit of Loneliness* (Beacon, 1970, $2.45).

Song Hits Magazine (Division Street, Derby, Connecticut 06418, $3.50 a year).

L. CLARK STEVENS, *EST: The Steersman Handbook* (Bantam, 1971, $1.50).

D. T. SUZUKI, *Studies in Zen* (Delta, 1955, $1.85).

PAUL SWATEK, *The User's Guide to the Protection of the Environment* (Friends of the Earth-Ballantine, 1970, $1.25).

JAY THOMPSON, *I Am Also a You* (Potter-Crown, 1971, $1.95).

HENRY DAVID THOREAU, *Walden* and *On the Duty of Civil Disobedience* (Collier, 1962 [1854, 1848], 65¢).

ALVIN TOFFLER, *Future Shock* (Bantam, 1971, $1.95).

SITA WEINER, *Swami Satchidananda* (Bantam, 1972 [1970], $1.95).

The Last Whole Earth Catalog (Portola Institute-Random House, 1971, $5.00).

ELIOT WIGGINTON (ed.), *The Foxfire Book* (Anchor, 1972, $3.95).

MASON WILLIAMS, *The Mason Williams FCC Rapport* (Liveright, 1969, $2.95).

TOM WOLFE, *The Electric Kool-Aid Acid Test* (Bantam, 1968, $1.25).

Acknowledgments

Television commercials are used throughout. There is no published compilation that can be cited. Most of those used here were obtained from advertising agency "story boards" on file with the Federal Trade Commission.

Page ii Lawrence Ferlinghetti, "I Am Waiting," *A Coney Island of the Mind* (1958) p. 49 / Howard Fast, *Citizen Tom Paine* (1943) pp. 30–31.

Page xx Mason Williams, "Commercials," *The Mason Williams FCC Rapport* (1969) p. 7.

Page 2 Rollo May, *Love and Will* (1969) p. 156 / Benjamin Spock, *Decent and Indecent—Our Personal and Political Behavior* (1969) p. 153 / Allen Ginsberg, quoted in *I Seem To Be A Verb* by R. Buckminster Fuller (1970) p. 165A / Archibald MacLeish, quoted in *Due to Circumstances Beyond Our Control* by Fred Friendly (1967) p. xxiv.

Page 3 *Report of the National Advisory Commission on Civil Disorders* (1968) Chapter 15 / David L. Lange, Robert K. Baker, Sandra J. Ball, *Violence and the Media: A Staff Report to the National Commission on the Causes and Prevention of Violence* (1969), vols. 9, 9A / Senator J. W. Fulbright, *The Pentagon Propaganda Machine* (1970).

Page 4 Andrew Fletcher, *Conversation Concerning a Right Regulation of Government for the Common Good of Mankind* (1703) / William F. Fore, *Image and Impact* (1970) p. 40 / Walter Lippmann, *Public Opinion* (1922) pp. 275–76.

Page 5 "Who's Afraid of Big Bad T.V.? *Time* (November 23, 1970) p. 60ff / "The Selling of the Candidates, 1970" *Newsweek* (November 19, 1970) p. 30ff / Robin Morgan, quoted in "Is Television Making a Mockery of the American Woman?" by Edith Efron, *TV Guide* (August 8, 1970) p. 6.

Page 6 Aurelio Peccei, "Problems of World Future," in *Technology Forecasting* (1970) pp. 229–33 / A Consumer Products Survey / Erich Fromm, *The Revolution of Hope* (1968) p. 153.

Page 7 *The New York Times* (July 13, 1970) p. 1 / U.S. Census, *Statistical Abstract of the United States* (1970) p. 712.

Page 8 Dr. William Glasser, "Youth in Rebellion—Why?" *U.S. News and World Report* (April 27, 1970) p. 42 / Arthur M. Schlesinger, Jr., "Velocity of History," *Newsweek* (July 6, 1970) p. 33 / The Mothers of Invention, "Hungry Freaks, Daddy," (1967) / Rollo May, *Man's Search for Himself* (1953) p. 22.

Page 9 U.S. Census, *Statistical Abstract of the United States* (1970) p. 50 / U.S. Census, *Statistical Abstract of the United States* (1970) p. 154 / "The American Family: Future Uncertain," *Time* (December 28, 1970) p. 34 / Joint Commission on Mental Health of Children, *Suicide Among Youth* (1969) / *The Movement Toward a New America*, edited by M. Goodman (1970) p. 101 / *The New York Times Encyclopedic Almanac* (1971) p. 500.

Page 10 Hermann Hesse, *Steppenwolf* (1929) p. 200 / Arnold S. Kaufman, *The Radical Liberal New Man in American Politics* (1968) p. 26 / R. D. Laing, *The Politics of Experience* (1967) pp. 25–26.

Page 12 Erich Fromm, *The Sane Society* (1955) p. 15 / Charles Manson, quoted in *Time* (November 30, 1970) p. 45 / Harvey Cox, *The Secular City* (1966, rev. ed.) p. 133 / Paul Goodman, *Growing Up Absurd* (1960) pp. 13–14.

Page 14 Ray Walczack, quoted in "The Troubled American: A Special Report of the White Majority," *Newsweek* (October 9, 1969) p. 57 / Joe South, "Don't It Make You Wanna Go Home?" (1969).

Page 16 Lawrence Ferlinghetti, "The World Is a Beautiful Place . . . ," *A Coney Island of the Mind* (1958) p. 88 / Marshall McLuhan, "Great Change-Overs for You," *Problems and Controversies in Television and Radio*, edited by H. T. Skornia and J. Kitson (1968) pp. 31–32 / Y. Yevtushenko, "Talk," *Selected Poems* (1962) p. 81.

Page 18 John V. Lindsay, Address at the University of California at Berkeley (April 2, 1970) / Richard J. Barnet, *Economy of Death* (1969) pp. 6–7 / Abraham Lincoln, Address, March 4, 1861, *Inaugural Addresses of Presidents of the United States*, U.S. Government Printing Office (1969) p. 125 / Milton Friedman, "The Social Responsibility of Business Is to Increase Its Profits," *The New York Times Magazine*

(September 13, 1970) p. 33 / Thomas C. Raymond, "The New Business Student," *Newsweek* (October 12, 1970) p. 76.

Page 20 E. Foote, Statement before the World Conference on Smoking and Health quoted in *To Seek a Newer World* by Robert Kennedy (1968) p. 6 / Alexander Kendrick, *Prime Time* (1969) p. 34 / Barry M. Goldwater, quoted in "The Politics of Ecology," by Wheeler, *Saturday Review* (March 7, 1970) p. 52 / Paddy Chayefsky, *The Latent Heterosexual* (1967) p. 105 / Richard J. Barnet, *The Economy of Death* (1969) p. 152.

Page 21 Nicholas Johnson, "Stewardess" (1972).

Page 22 Country Joe McDonald, "I-Feel-Like-I'm-Fixing-To-Die-Rag," (1968) / J. Brown, B. Byrd and R. Lenhoff, "Get Up, Get Into It, Get Involved," (1970) / Patrick Watson, *Conspirators in Silence* (1969) p. 59 / Erik Barnouw, *The Image Empire* (1970) p. 343.

Page 24 William F. Fore, *Image and Impact* (1970) pp. 45–46 / Philip Slater, *The Pursuit of Loneliness* (1970) p. 14.

Page 26 Timothy J. Cooney and James Haughton, *It's up to You: A Guide to Changing the System* (1971) pp. 97–98.

Page 28 David Riesman, *Abundance for What? And Other Essays* (1964) p. 180 / Spiro T. Agnew, "Another Challenge to the Television Industry," *TV Guide* (May 16, 1970) p. 8 / Suzannah Lessard, "America's Traps: The Youth Cult, The Work Prison, The Emptiness of Age," *The Washington Monthly* (February, 1971) p. 31 / Mason Williams, *Flavors* (1970).

Page 30 Mason Williams, *The Mason Williams Reading Matter* (1969) / Paul Swatek, *The User's Guide in the Protection of the Environment* (1970) p. 9.

Page 32 Richard M. Nixon, quoted in *The Washington Post* (November 12, 1969) p. B15 / George F. Kennan, "Con III Is Not the Answer," *The New York Times* (November 28, 1970) p. 43 / Robert L. Shayon, "T.V. and Radio: Father Television Knows Best," *Saturday Review* (December 5, 1964) p. 42 / Melanie Safka, "What Have They Done to My Song, Ma," (1970).

Page 34 Jerry Rubin, *Do It!* (1970) p. 87 / Gene Maclellan, "Put Your Hand in the Hand," (1970) / Warren Magnuson, *The Television Inquiry*, Senate Committee on Commerce, 89th Congress, 2nd Session, Senate No. 2769, From Letter of Transmittal to Federal Communications Commission iv (1956).

Page 36 James Kunen, *The Strawberry Statement* (1970) p. 79 / Walter Cronkite, quoted in "Television: The Most Intimate Medium," *Time* (October 14, 1966) p. 57 / Frank N. Stanton and Paul F. Lazarsfeld, *Introduction to Communication Research* (1949) p. xii / David Sarnoff, *Looking Ahead* (1968) pp. 39–40 / William Benton, "Television With a Conscience," *Saturday Review* (August 25, 1951) p. 7.

Page 38 E. B. White, Letter from E. B. White to the Carnegie Commission on Educational Television, *Public Television, A Program for Action* (1967) p. 13 / Walter Lippmann, quoted in *Due to Circumstances Beyond Our Control*, by Fred Friendly (1967) p. 116 / Mason Williams, *The Mason Williams FCC Rapport* (1969) p. 136 / Richard M. Nixon, remarks at White House Bi-Partisan Leadership Meeting (October 23, 1969) / George Clayton Johnson, "An Open Letter to CBS," *Los Angeles Free Press* (May 15, 1970).

Page 40 Tim Buckley, "Goodbye and Hello," (1968) / Erik Barnouw, *The Image Empire* (1970) p. 33.

Page 42 William F. Fore, *Image and Impact* (1970) p. 40.

Page 44 Rice, "The Biography of A Play," *Theatre Arts* (November, 1969) / William F. Fore, *Image and Impact* (1970) pp. 48–49 / Eve Merriam, "On Teevee," *The Inner City Mother Goose* (1969) p. 79.

Page 46 Robert H. Finch, Address to the Television Bureau of Advertising, 15th Annual Meeting (October 21, 1969) / Clyde Miller, quoted in *The Hidden Persuaders* by Vance Packard (1957) pp. 158–59 / William F. Fore, *Image and Impact* (1970) p. 17 / Wilbur Schramm, quoted in *Television in the Lives of Our Children*, edited by W. Schramm, E. Parker, and J. Lyle (1961) p. 58.

Page 48 Marian Delgado, Remarks at CBS Annual Meeting of Shareholders, San Francisco (April 15, 1970) / Donna Keck, "The Art of Maiming Women," *Women, A Journal of Liberation* (Fall, 1969) p. 42.

Page 50 Robin Morgan, quoted in "Is Television Making a Mockery of the American Woman?" by Edith Efron, *TV Guide* (August 8, 1970) p. 8 / Norman Mark, "TV's Sexual Guard Isn't Very Avant," *Chicago*

Daily News (Panorama, July 18–19, 1970) p. 19 / Dr. Mary S. Caldecrone, "Sex and the Communicative Arts," speech delivered to *Seventeen* magazine's major advertisers, "Seventeen's Think Young Think Tank," New York (September 11, 1969) / Rollo May, *Man's Search for Himself* (1953) p. 145.

Page 51 Nicholas Johnson, "Sex" (1972).

Page 52 Larry Niven, "Death by Ecstasy," *The World's Best Science Fiction*, edited by D. Wollheim and T. Carr (1970) pp. 50–51 / Mick Jagger and Keith Richard, "(I Can't Get No) Satisfaction," (1962).

Page 54 R. Buckminster Fuller, quoted in "Open Land," by S. Davidson, *Harper's* (June, 1970) p. 100 / Joni Mitchell, "Woodstock," (1969) / Glenn Yarbrough, quoted in "Singer Chucks Fame, Wealth for Simple Life," by D. Lamb, *Los Angeles Times* (February 21, 1971) p. 1 / Henry David Thoreau, *Walden* (1854, Collier 1962) p. 74.

Page 56 Helen and Scott Nearing, *Living the Good Life* (1970) p. 186.

Page 58 Alicia Bay Laurel, *Living on the Earth* (1970), Introduction / Roger J. Williams, "The Biology of Behavior," *Saturday Review* (January 30, 1971) / Henry David Thoreau, *Walden* (1854, Collier 1962) p. 106.

Page 60 R. Self, "What Every Little Boy Ought to Know," (1970) / Mason Williams, *The Mason Williams FCC Rapport* (1969) p. 95 / W. H. Auden, "Forgotten Laughter, Forgotten Prayer," *The New York Times* (February 2, 1971) p. 37.

Page 62 Rainer Maria Rilke, *Letters to a Young Poet* (rev. ed. 1954) p. 19 / Margaret Lewis and Mira Smith, "Oh, Singer," (1971) / Rollo May, *Man's Search for Himself* (1953) p. 137 / *Bhagavad Gita*, 2:71.

Page 64 Mac Davis, "Everything a Man Could Ever Need," (1969, 1970) / Holderlin, *The Movement Toward a New America*, edited by Mitchell Goodman (1970) p. 25 / Roger J. Williams, "The Biology of Behavior," *Saturday Review* (January 30, 1971) p. 17 / Rainer Maria Rilke, *Letters to a Young Poet* (rev. ed. 1954) pp. 53–54 / Betty Craig, "Money Can't Buy Love," (1970).

Page 66 Staughton Lynd, "Again—Don't Tread On Me," *Newsweek* (July 6, 1970) p. 31 / James A. Michener, *The Quality of Life* (1970) p. 116 / Edward A. Sapir, "Culture, Genuine and Spurious," *Selected Writings of Edward Sapir*, edited by David Mandelbaum (1949) p. 323.

Page 68 Ou Yang Hsiu, "Reading the Poem of An Absent Friend," *One Hundred Poems From the Chinese*, edited by Kenneth Rexroth (1965) pp. 57, 58 / Hermann Hesse, *Steppenwolf* (1963) p. 144 / Ralph Waldo Emerson, "Illusions," *The Portable Emerson*, edited by M. Van Doren (1969) pp. 234–35 / Henry David Thoreau, *Walden* (1854, Collier 1962) p. 22 / *The Book of Tao* 29, D. Goddard, ed., *A Buddhist Bible* (1938) p. 418.

Page 70 Edward A. Sapir, "Culture, Genuine and Spurious," *Selected Writings of Edward Sapir*, edited by David Mandelbaum (1949) p. 316 / Sara Davidson, "Open Land," *Harper's* (June, 1970) p. 100 / Erich Fromm, *Revolution of Hope* (1968) p. 1 / Edmund Carpenter, "Art As Act," *They Became What They Beheld* (1970) unpaged.

Pages 72, 74, 76 Art Buchwald, "The Great TV Blackout," *The Washington Post* (February 16, 1971) p. C-1.

Page 76 Edmund Carpenter, "Art As Act," *They Become What They Beheld* (1970) unpaged / Former United Air Lines labor relations executive, quoted in "The Great Escape—Leaving the Security of a Corporate Payroll," by John Koehne. *Wall Street Journal* (February 22, 1971) p. 1.

Page 78 Bobby Bond, "Back to Where It's At," (1970) / Ann-Elizabeth, "The Experiment," *The Magic Book of Love Exercises* (1971) p. 29 / Ralph Waldo Emerson, "Illusions," *The Portable Emerson*, edited by M. Van Doren (1969) p. 27.

Page 80 John Hartford, "Baking Soda," *Word Movies* (1971) p. 42 / Paul Swatek, *The User's Guide to the Protection of the Environment* (1970) p. 93.

Page 82 John Prine, "Spanish Pipe Dream," (1971).

Page 84 Philip Slater, *The Pursuit of Loneliness* (1970) p. 93.

Page 86 Adelle Davis, *Let's Eat Right to Keep Fit* (1970) p. 63 / Dr. George A. Sheehan, quoted in article in *Chicago Tribune* by Robert Lipsyte.

Page 88 Adelle Davis, *Let's Eat Right To Keep Fit* (1970) p. 16.

Page 90   Walter Sullivan, "Meteor Findings Back Theory on Life," *The New York Times* (June 19, 1971) p. 28 / Robert Choate, "Television Ads Aimed at Children Stir Ire of Parents, Critics," *The Wall Street Journal* (October 22, 1970) p. 1.

Page 92   "Pauling Asserts Large Doses of Vitamin C Can Prevent Colds," *The New York Times* (November 19, 1970).

Page 94   Marcia Cavell, "Visions of a New Religion," *Saturday Review* (December 19, 1970) p. 12 / Joan Baez, *Daybreak* (1968) pp. 137–38 / John Koehne, "The Great Escape—Leaving the Security of the Corporate Payroll," *The Wall Street Journal* (February 22, 1971) p. 1.

Page 96   Nobutane Kiuchi, "Japan Will Have to Slow Down," *Fortune* (February, 1971) p. 98 / Rainer Maria Rilke, *Letters to a Young Poet* (1954, rev. ed.) p. 30 / Walter McQuade, "High Style Disrupts the Men's Wear Industry," *Fortune* (February, 1971) p. 70.

Page 98   Bernadine Morris, "Beachwear? Streetwear? It's All Starting to Look the Same," *The New York Times* (June 19, 1971) p. C 14 / Karl Fleming, "The Square American Speaks Out," *Newsweek* (October 6, 1969) p. 50 / E. B. White, "Commuter," *The Lady Is Cold* (1925).

Page 100   Jules Henry, *Culture Against Man* (1963) p. 95 / Philip Slater, "The Pursuit of Loneliness," *Psychology Today* (July, 1970) John Hartford, "The Good Old Electric Washing Machine Circa 1943," *Word Movies* (1971) pp. 117–18.

Page 102   Garrett DeBell, "Energy," *The Environmental Handbook* (1970) pp. 66–67 / Paul Swatek, *The User's Guide to the Protection of the Environment* (1970) p. 39.

Page 104   Betty Ann Ottinger, *What Every Woman Should Know and Do About Pollution* (1970) pp. 66–67 / Joni Mitchell, "Big Yellow Taxi," (1970) / Betty Ann Ottinger, *What Every Woman Should Know and Do About Pollution* (1970) pp. 59–60 / Bill Scudder, quoted in "The Troubled American: A Report on the White Majority," *Newsweek* (October 6, 1969) p. 59.

Page 106   L. Clark Stevens, *EST* (1970) pp. 132–33 / John Holt, "School Is Bad for Children," *Saturday Evening Post* (February 8, 1969) p. 269 / G. Ragni and J. Rado, *Hair* (1969) p. 86 / Aaron Copland. *What to Listen for in Music* (1957) p. 24.

Page 108   Robert A. Heinlein, *Stranger in a Strange Land* (1961) p. 382 / Rainer Maria Rilke, *Letters to a Young Poet* (1954, rev. ed.) p. 74.

Page 110   C. E. Warne, "No Time to Live," address before Unitarian Forum, Kansas City, Mo. (October 7, 1951) / R. Buckminster Fuller, *Operating Manual for Spaceship Earth* (1969) pp. 129–30 / MG advertisement in *Time* (March 6, 1970) p. 6.

Page 112   Paul Swatek, *The User's Guide to the Protection of the Environment* (1970) pp. 285–86 / Edward T. Hall, quoted in *The Environmental Handbook*, edited by G. DeBell (1970) p. 199.

Page 114   Paul Swatek, *The User's Guide to the Protection of the Environment* (1970) pp. 253, 285–86.

Page 116   Thomas R. Reid III, "Easy Rider: A Solution to the Commuter Crisis," Vol. 116 *Congressional Record* p. 55868 (April 16, 1970) / Friends of the Earth, "National Bike Week," *Man Apart* (April, 1972) p. 3.

Page 118   Rollo May, *Man's Search for Himself* (1953) p. 42 / John Gardner, *The Recovery of Confidence* (1970) p. 77 / Louis B. Lundborg, "The Lessons of Isla Vista," speech to Seattle Rotary Club (June 17, 1970).

Page 120   Seymour Melman, *Our Depleted Society* (1965) p. 128 / A welder and Willie Sanders, quoted in "The Square American Speaks Out," by Karl Fleming, *Newsweek* (October 6, 1969) p. 50.

Page 122   Erich Fromm, *Revolution of Hope* (1968) p. 125.

Page 124   David Broder, *Parade* (February 15, 1970) p. 23 / Former New York stockbroker and former insurance man, quoted in "The Great Escape—Leaving the Security of the Corporate Payroll Isn't Easy," by John Koehne, *Wall Street Journal* (February 22, 1971) p. 1.

Page 126   Former corporate engineer, quoted in "The Great Escape—Leaving the Security of a Corporate Payroll Isn't Easy," by John Koehne, *Wall Street Journal* (February 22, 1971) p. 1 / Taylor Branch, "Courage Without Esteem: Profiles in Whistle Blowing," *Washington Monthly* (May, 1971) p. 36.

Page 128 Suzannah Lessard, "America's Trap: The Youth Cult, The Work Prison, The Emptiness of Age," *The Washington Monthly* (February, 1971) p. 30 / Archibald MacLeish, "Speech To A Crowd," *The Collected Poems of Archibald MacLeish* (1962) p. 115 / Elie Wiesel, "To a Young Rebel," *The Washington Post* (February 18, 1971) p. C 1.

Page 130 Charles A. Reich, *The Greening of America* (1970) pp. 429, 430 / Howard Zinn, "The Radicals: Time Out to Retrench," *Time* (February 22, 1971) p. 10.

Page 132 Jerry Edmonton, John Day and Nick St. Nicholas, "Monster," (1970) / Barry Mann and Cynthia Weil, "New World Coming," (1970).

Page 133 *The New York Times* (December 26, 1970) p. 14 / "The American Family: Future Uncertain," *Time* (December 28, 1970) p. 27 / Source Coalition, Washington, D.C., *Source Catalogue Communications*, 1971 / U.S. Public Health Service.

Page 134 Gil Scott-Heron, "The Revolution Will Not Be Televised," (1970) / William O. Douglas, *Points of Rebellion*, p. 96 / Martin Luther King, Jr., quoted in "The Radicals: Time Out To Retrench," by J. Bernbaum, *Time* (February 22, 1971) p. 10.

Page 135 The Singer Sewing Machine Company / *Everybody's Money* (Winter 1970–71) p. 12 / U.S. Public Health Service.

Page 136 A gas station attendant, quoted in "The Average Man Might Fool You," by Robert Coles, *Life* (May 7, 1971) p. 4 / Fred Harris, David Frost Show broadcast in Washingtin, D.C., WTTG–TV (July 17, 1970) / A policeman, quoted in "The Average Man Might Fool You," by Robert Coles, *Life* (May 7, 1971) p. 4 / Edward M. Kennedy, *Decisions for a Decade* (1968).

Page 138 Melanie Safka, "Nickel Song," (1970) / Mayer Vishner, "Editor's Afterword: The Role of Rock," *1971 Peace Calendar* (1970) / Paul Goodman, *The New York Times* (September 2, 1970) p. 32 / Red Lane, Larry Henley, and Johnny Slate, "The World Needs a Melody," (1971).

Page 140 Louis B. Lundborg, "The Lessons of Isla Vista," speech to Seattle Rotary Club (June 17, 1970) / Edward H. Meyer, "Grey Matter," *Consumer Reports* (November, 1970).

Page 142 Stanley Cohen, quoted in "Advertising on the Defensive in the Age of Disbelief," by Coleman McCarthy, *The Washington Post* (November 8, 1970) p. B 3.

Credits

During 1970–72 a number of persons in my family, the Bantam family, my office, and elsewhere assisted in a variety of ways to bring me, and this book, into being. They know who they are, and what they did. Some are listed here—alphabetically by first names—as a token of my appreciation, debt, or love, as the case may be.

Al, Andi, Andy, Angela, Anne, Bob, Bonnie, Candy, Carlos, Carol, Catherine, Charles, Cheri, Chet, Chris, Craig, Debbie, Denny, Don, Donna, Doris, Ed, Edna, Elaine, Elizabeth, Esther, Evie, Florrie, Fran, Fred, Gary, Gilson, Gregory, Hank, Hans, Harriet, Hildegard, Jack, Jane, Jean, Jeff, Jeneen, Jenny, Jerry, Jim, Joe, Judy, Julie, Karen, Katy, Lee, Leni, Linda, Liz, Lucy, Marc, Margo, Marlene, Marv, Mary Ann, Mason, Max, Mel, Meredith, Michael, Pat, Peggy, Phil, Ralph, Rich, Sam, Sharon, Sherman, Stephan, Stephanie, Susan, Thorper, Tom, Toni, Tracy, Vic, Willa, Wretha.

Sources

Some of the ideas contained in this book were first presented in the Pauly Ballroom, University of California, Berkeley, November 7, 1970, as the annual Barbara Weinstock Lecture on the Morals of Trade. The text of that speech was published in a limited edition by the University of California as *Life Before Death in the Corporate State* (1971).

The speech was recorded for broadcast, and is available to radio stations from the Pacifica Tape Library (2217 Shattuck Avenue, Berkeley, California 94704 [no. AP1369]).

Ten brief excerpts were distributed to radio stations by American Report (Clergy and Laymen Concerned, P. O. Box 6676, Washington, D. C. 20009) as its May 8–20, 1972 bi-weekly, recorded distribution of daily programs.

Elektra Records plans to release an LP based upon the speech entitled "Test Pattern for Living."

Some of the ideas come from a speech presented as a Poynter Fellow Lecture at Yale University on March 8, 1971 under the title, "The Careening of America."

A third public performance, at Grinnell College on April 1, 1971, was televised by the Iowa Educational Broadcasting Network on April 12, 1971 under the title "How to Survive in a Corporate Society."

The title "Test Pattern for Living" was first used in an article published in the *Saturday Review*, May 29, 1971, pages 12–15 and 33.

That article was recorded for the blind and distributed by *Choice Magazine Listening* (125 Main Street, Port Washington, New York 10050), Issue 57, Sides 1 and 2, September 1971.

Other material is drawn from "The Life Party," *The New Republic*, April 10, 1971, pages 21–23, and a commencement address at Windham College, "Working in a Corporate State," May 23, 1971.

Although the author has received no payment for any presentation of this material, and will receive no royalties from this book, he wishes to express his appreciation to those who have provided the prior occasions to prepare it, who have taken an interest in its distribution, and who have granted such permissions as were necessary on this occasion.

ABOUT THE AUTHOR

NICHOLAS JOHNSON was born in Iowa City in 1934, and earned B.A. and LL.B. degrees from the University of Texas (Austin) where he was Phi Beta Kappa and a student editor of the *Texas Law Review*. He has served as a law clerk to Chief Judge John R. Brown of the U.S. Court of Appeals (5th Circuit) and to senior Associate Justice Hugo L. Black of the U.S. Supreme Court, and as a member of the law faculty at the University of California (Berkeley). He was an associate member of the Washington, D.C. law firm, Covington & Burling, when appointed U.S. Maritime Administrator by President Lyndon B. Johnson in 1964. His seven-year term as an FCC Commissioner began on July 1, 1966. One of the youngest men ever to hold these positions, he was selected by the U.S. Jaycees as one of the nation's "Ten Outstanding Young Men" in 1967. He has written for many general and professional publications and is the author of *How to Talk Back to Your Television Set*.